RUNNING YOUR OWN BOARDING KENNELS

Feline Advisory Bureau
Full page Colour

RUNNING YOUR OWN BOARDING KENNELS

The Complete Guide to Kennel and Cattery Management

REVISED 4TH EDITION

DAVID CAVILL

KOGAN PAGE

Publisher's note

Every possible effort has been made to ensure that the information contained in this book is accurate at the time of going to press, and the publishers and author cannot accept responsibility for any errors or omissions, however caused. No responsibility for loss or damage occasioned to any person acting, or refraining from action, as a result of the material in this publication can be accepted by the editor, the publisher or the author.

First published in 1985
Reprinted with revisions 1986, 1988
Second edition 1992
Reprinted with revisions 1997
Reprinted 1999
Third edition 2002
Reprinted 2004
Fourth edition 2005
Reprinted 2006, 2008
Revised fourth edition 2008

Kogan Page Limited
120 Pentonville Road
London N1 9JN
www.koganpage.com

British Library Cataloguing in Publication Data

A CIP record for this book is available from the British Library.

ISBN 978 0 7494 5330 5

Typeset by Jean Cussons Typesetting, Diss, Norfolk
Printed and bound in Great Britain by Thanet Press Ltd, Margate

Contents

Pedigree Pens Ltd
Full page colour

Pedgree Pens Ltd
1 page Edit

Acknowledgements

I gratefully acknowledge the help, encouragement and advice given me by many people including Mr David Cavill of the Bellmead Kennel Staff Training College, the late Miss S M Hamilton Moore, former Boarding Cattery Officer of the Feline Advisory Bureau, Mr Trevor Turner, MRCVS, Dr Alan Walker, Mr Vincent Hogan and Mr William Moores of Our Dogs, Mr Tony Ellis and Miss Carol Andrews of Kennel and Cattery Management, and Mr Jerry Brownlee of Pet Plan Insurance Ltd. My particular thanks go to Mrs Brenda Judson, Mrs Jill Ashwick, and also to Wendy and Graham Stephens of Arden Grange International Quarantine and Boarding Kennels for their practical advice as experienced kennel owners. I am extremely grateful to Monica and David Marshall for allowing me to share their initiation into the world of boarding kennel ownership, and who have continued to make me welcome on frequent visits to their now well-established kennel business.

Sheila Zabawa
September 1991

Sheila's acknowledgements cover most of those who have helped me in the extensive revision of her work. However, I must add Christopher Armstrong, Heather Briggs, Pam Gee, Sue Hawkins, David Key and Barry Huckle to the list, as well as a general thank you to my wife Angela and the wonderful staff who have worked with me in the industry over the last 30 years.

David Cavill
June 2008

Foreword

So you want to run a kennel and/or a cattery? I was asked to write this foreword because I have searched for, purchased, rebuilt and operated a boarding kennel and cattery. I can identify with the many considerations that a prospective purchaser faces.

Running a boarding establishment is very rewarding but no easy option. Before embarking on this road you will need to spend a significant amount of time in considering and researching the project, and you will need advice.

I believe the process starts with self-analysis and asking yourself the following questions: Do I have the stamina and good health to cope with the pressure and long hours of a physically demanding 365-days-a-year task? Do I have a sufficiently robust personality to cope with an increasingly discerning general public and with customers who may be difficult? Do I have business acumen? Do I have the patience to listen politely to customers telling me about their animals? Do I have experience in the relentless routine of caring for animals? Have I undertaken training to gain qualifications in kennel and cattery management? Do I have well-developed organisation skills? Do I have basic accounting ability and information technology skills? Am I conscientious and do I have the knowledge and dedication to care for the complex needs of the boarders who will be my responsibility? Will family and other demands allow me to take on such a major commitment?

If you can answer yes to all of the above, then go on to consider how you will find your kennels and cattery and how you will finance the project.

The industry is in a period of slow but major change. Years ago it was a cottage industry but it is gradually moving towards larger and more professionally run establishments. Although Model Licence Conditions were introduced in 1995 to set standards, many establishments still fall far short of what should be provided. Improvement is slowly coming and is being driven more by customer expectation than by regulations.

It is essential when sizing up a potential purchase that due provision is made for rebuilding or modernisation costs where necessary. Such costs may be significant and the income may not be sufficient to finance refurbishment, particularly if there are also loan repayments to be made. In short, you need a properly constructed business plan. Finding kennels or a cattery that you desire will not be easy and location is a vital factor. You do need to be adjacent to a sizeable centre of population to draw year-round trade.

If the above points have provoked thought, then they have achieved their aim. What should you do to further explore these points? The answer is to thoroughly read this book. It offers a wealth of distilled experience. It will help you decide if this really is for you and will guide you through the hurdles you will face and help you to avoid the pitfalls. It is essential reading if you are to be successful and I commend it to you.

Christopher Armstrong
Chilworth Boarding Kennels and Cattery, Southampton

Burns Pet Nutrition Ltd
Full page colour

Burns Pet Nutrition Ltd
1 of 2 edit

Burns Pet Nutrition Ltd
2 of 2 edit

1 Facing the Facts

Before considering the purchase of a boarding kennel it is important to ask yourself and your family, 'Will life in a boarding kennel suit us?' It is vital to pause for thought and try to give yourselves an honest answer, for many people wishing to enter the animal care industry have had little or no experience of small animal boarding establishments and therefore have not very much on which to base their answers. It is an occupation of great responsibility involving the complete care of other people's pets, and a kind, caring and understanding attitude towards animals and a sympathetic approach to their owners is essential.

Dogs and cats, and possibly some other small animals, become residents of a boarding kennel intermittently for varying periods. The kennel owners live there permanently, and although their personal accommodation is somewhat more spacious, they also face certain restrictions when assuming a 24 hours a day, seven days a week, responsibility for their clients' pets. Naturally, there are compensations and every aspect needs to be weighed carefully before embarking on a venture which is demanding both in capital investment and physical endurance, but which can be highly rewarding in terms of satisfaction, provided the kennel owners are suited to their work, and can make the most of its advantages and tolerate its disadvantages.

Boarding kennels are extremely individual businesses and offer self-employment, freedom from a deskbound job, an outdoor life and, it would seem, stable employment as people tend to take more holidays than in the past and therefore need boarding facilities for their pets more frequently. Despite the increased flexibility resulting from what has become known as the Pets Passport scheme, this is also an era in which restrictions on dogs have become more severe. Shops, beaches, hotels, caravan parks, self-catering holiday flats or chalets and public parks have become 'off limits' to dogs, or are so stringent in their restrictions that visitors taking their pets into strange areas find their own vacations spoiled. It is far better for the family pet to go to its own holiday camp – your boarding kennel! Many boarding kennels are now finding that they have bookings all the year round as winter holidays are becoming universally popular, and weekend breaks, which are extensively advertised, are attracting people who have the leisure to enjoy them.

Nevertheless, some parts of the year will definitely see the kennels more empty than others and careful planning is needed in the early days of ownership to cover the financially lean periods. Freedom from constant clerical work does not mean that there are no desk jobs at all. Accounts must be kept, bookings made, a register of boarders maintained and, particularly while you are gaining experience, investigations into all aspects of running the business profitably need to be continued. The outdoor life, which can be very enjoyable when the weather is beautiful, must be endured when it is inclement beyond description; it is not easy to enjoy working outside in torrents of rain but the basic tasks still need to be done.

A flair for DIY is a definite, perhaps even an essential, asset to any boarding kennel owner. There are always maintenance and alteration jobs, as some dogs while away their happy holiday hours destroying whatever their teeth and claws can reach, and there is usually something in a kennel block which might be better for some modification. If a kennel owner is a competent plumbing and heating engineer and an expert in drains, as well as a capable electrician, so much the better! However, many folk of slight physical strength and deficient in DIY aptitude become extremely successful boarding kennel owners. Profitable kennel ownership may well be a triumph over adversity, and what constitutes a serious problem for one owner may be a mere bagatelle for the next.

Boarding establishments for family pets are sometimes part of a breeding and exhibiting kennel. Usually, dog or cat breeding or exhibiting has led the owner into the boarding business because it appears to be an easy and economic way to fund their hobby. In such cases the owner may have acquired considerable experience of animals in a kennel environment before assuming the care of other people's pets. However, those who wish to follow the exhibition lure will find that show dates conflict with the busiest boarding season, necessitating complicated staffing arrangements, and, though exhibiting at dog or cat shows can be a compelling interest, it is not in itself a paying occupation. It costs money, even for the glory of winning at prestigious shows. Show entries can be expensive, prize money nil and travel costs exorbitant, not to mention extra staff salaries if members of the family are not available to cope on the home front while others are away at shows. Remember that pet owners, when leaving or collecting their dogs and cats, expect to be met by competent adults; if a boarding kennel owner is not available to attend to the clients personally, it is essential for the confidence of the clients and the goodwill of the establishment that whoever meets them makes a good impression. You cannot afford to leave a school-age youngster in charge. Can you and your family give yourselves wholeheartedly to the business, particularly in the early days of ownership?

A SECOND CAREER

Many people come into the boarding kennel business as a second career with the advantage of business or professional experience and training, and a certain maturity. This is almost inevitable, as the capital cost is high. Boarding kennel ownership also attracts some people already qualified in animal care. Veterinary surgeons sometimes own kennels and obviously have many professional advantages; veterinary nurses are often interested in kennel ownership and again have definite advantages of training and experience. Members of the armed forces, many of whom retire from the services in their middle years, quite frequently find the ownership of animal boarding establishments an interesting and practical pursuit. Years of training, discipline and an outdoor life, plus dependability and self-sufficiency, are a commendable background. Men and women from all walks of life are interested in animal care, and many find that the boarding kennel business appears to offer them the ideal occupation.

Those choosing kennel ownership as a second career usually have ample time to consider possibilities and prepare for the tasks involved. When life has not previously included specific training in animal welfare, how should prospective kennel owners proceed?

GAINING THE KNOWLEDGE

If you can, it would be sensible to obtain some practical experience in the sector, but in any case you must become as well informed as possible on all subjects relevant to small animal care. How can this be achieved? The internet is a great source of information with many good websites – a lot of which are mentioned in this book. Another way is to benefit from the peripheral activities connected with the exhibition community, which is closer knit than the boarding kennel world.

The exhibition scene, through its excellent publications, provides a wealth of necessary background information and general reading material of interest to intending kennel owners. In particular, the weekly canine journals print up-to-date news concerning changes in legislation, and carry advertising material which is most useful.

One bi-monthly journal, *Kennel and Cattery Management*, is aimed specifically at the boarding sector and contains informative articles on all subjects relating to small animal boarding. Other canine and feline journals encompass the show and breeding world as well as publishing items of interest for boarding kennel owners. People who plan to become the owners of boarding establishments should certainly become regular readers of such weekly papers as *Our Dogs*, and its sister magazine *Our Cats*, and *Dog World*, all obtainable to order from newsagents nationwide.

Intending boarding kennel owners, though they may not be interested in showing dogs themselves, should read the forthcoming show announcements in *Our Dogs* and *Dog World* if only to be aware of what is going on in their own area. They give details of shows nationwide for exhibitors making entries in advance, and list current events for intending spectators. Many people have the false idea that Crufts is the only dog show! There is sure to be a dog or cat show at some time in your present neighbourhood, or at least within a reasonable travelling distance. Attending local shows could help you to become more familiar with breeds of dogs and cats you may never have encountered but might at some time board. Championship dog and cat shows attract the highest number of entries and stands dealing in kennel necessities, so trade sections are worth visiting too. Separate trade fairs are also interesting, and advertisements for them will be found in the weekly dog press and in the monthly magazines *Pet Product Marketing* and *Pet Business News*.

However, the first port of call should be the Pet Care Trust, www.petcare.org.uk. Formerly the Pet Trade and Industry Association, the Trust represents kennel and cattery owners to government and to local authorities, monitors legislation likely to effect all those involved in the animal care industry and circulates that information to its members. It also provides a whole range of other legal and financial services and advice that kennel owners will find useful and includes regular surveys of pay, conditions, boarding fees and licence fees. A dedicated board member of the Trust represents the industry and chairs a panel of experienced owners that meets when necessary to ensure the organisation fully represents their interests. The Trust also publishes a Code of Conduct and a Boarding Kennels and Catteries Manual that new owners will find extremely helpful. Most important, membership includes insurance cover for legal expenses – vital in an increasingly litigious world and the recent activities of some branches of the RSPCA Inspectorate.

The noise factor

Dogs bark! A superfluous statement? Not really. One of the most important questions intending boarding kennel owners must ask themselves is,

'Can I tolerate a high level of noise?' Naturally, barking cannot be prevented, and though good management may keep the noise level in check, there will be some extremely noisy spells. Noise is a stress factor and can be very wearing at times. For some people it is unbearable. Boarding kennel owners must learn to live with it, or live elsewhere. Recent health and safety discussions in the services have focused on the possible damage to hearing of kennel staff. No doubt this will impact on commercial boarding kennels in time.

Unpleasant smells and dirty jobs

Boarding kennel owners also have to accept other unavoidable facts: kennel work is very strenuous, and the dirty and tiresome jobs, as well as the more enjoyable tasks, have to be done.

Can you tolerate nasty smells? This question has to be answered truthfully. Although you may consider that all household pets will be house-trained, your kennel routine will be different from their home surroundings and the dogs will not understand at first why they have been handed over to you. Also, the smell of other dogs may set off their reactions and home toilet training may be temporarily forgotten.

There will be dirty kennels to cope with on most days, and in quarantine, where dogs are confined to the same kennel and adjoining exercise area for the duration of their detention, there will always be dirty kennels to clean and disinfect. If you cannot face unpleasant smells, you cannot face a kennel job, and you must be honest with yourself about these basic problems.

ANIMAL NURSING

Although the boarding kennel business attracts people who have had animal nursing experience, many newcomers to the trade will have had no dealings with sick animals, or even those with chronic conditions needing regular medication. Unless a boarding kennel owner is competent in caring for ailing animals he or she must recommend their owners to another kennel or to a veterinary surgeon. There are dogs which are diabetic and need daily treatment; dogs with a pancreatic deficiency may need a special diet routine; there are dogs with kidney disorders, arthritic and dysplastic dogs, very young dogs, aged dogs... all possible subjects for nursing care. Can you give this? Could you learn to give such care? Giving pills to dogs and cats is not always easy and the apparently simple logistics of ensuring that the correct medication is given to the right dog in the right quantity at the appropriate time can be a nightmare if you are not properly organised.

PRACTICAL PREPARATION

The acquisition of practical experience of kennel work for a second career may not be easy unless you are prepared to sacrifice some of your leisure to work in a voluntary capacity, perhaps for an animal charity. If you can manage it, it is well worth doing for many reasons. Contact your local branch of the Royal Society for the Prevention of Cruelty to Animals (RSPCA, www.rspca.org.uk), or the Dogs Trust (www dogstrust.org.uk) and enquire whether they could use a helping hand. There may possibly be an independent local animal sanctuary needing help; consult the Yellow Pages under 'Boarding Kennels' for information.

It may also be possible to help out voluntarily at a local boarding kennel or cattery, or perhaps you have friends already established in the business who would be pleased to assist with your indoctrination. It would be a good plan to see as many kennels as possible, but remember that kennel owners are extremely busy people; they are working when they may seem to you to be simply standing and watching! Show courtesy and consideration, and always make an appointment in advance. Be as understanding of them as you hope others will be of you in the future. Friends who are established owners are in a position to point out small matters of importance that the uninitiated may not otherwise see.

FORMAL TRAINING

Fortunately, recent years have seen great strides in opportunities for people interested in working with animals in the boarding environment to gain formal education. They can now study for the Diploma of Kennel Management which is organised and administered by the Animal Care College, Index House, Ascot, Berkshire SL5 7EU, www.animalcare college.co.uk, e-mail: acc@rtc-mail.org.uk; the course organisers will send full details on application. Study time is 180 hours. Beware of those who might encourage you to think that you can learn everything there is to know in a weekend! The college is a member of, and accredited by, the Open College Network and is also a member of the British Association of Correspondence Colleges.

The advent of formal study courses in boarding kennel management and other aspects of pet care such as nutrition and first aid is not only a great help to students but should set a higher standard and ensure a better professional image for small animal boarding establishments nationwide. Although not required by law, the new Model Licence Conditions, covered in detail later, place great emphasis on qualifications and training. Formal qualifications are therefore highly desirable and may be influential in certain circumstances – in the case of a dispute, for example.

THE BOARDING CATTERY

So far, in referring to small animal boarding establishments, those catering for dogs *and* cats have been mentioned. It should be noted that cats are better suited to care in a cattery exclusively for their own kind, and there are many such establishments, a few of which come on to the market annually. Occasionally, it may be possible to acquire permission to start a new cattery where a dog boarding kennel would not be allowed. It is essential that someone starting or taking over a cattery has both practical and theoretical training before accepting other people's cats to board.

The fact that cats are in general smaller than dogs, that they are all of similar size and that most pet cats are neutered so the sex problems of a dog boarding kennel are avoided, are no reasons at all for considering cat boarding as the easier and more lucrative option, and the suggestion is to be deplored. Cats are sensitive, selective and fastidious; close proximity to canine boarders is a great strain on them.

Though cats ideally should be boarded separately from dogs, we do not live in an ideal world. Some pet owners who have both animals prefer to take them to the same boarding kennel, perhaps for personal convenience or possibly because they are not aware of the desirability of separate boarding for each species. It is also more likely that the owner of a dog boarding kennel would be granted permission to add a cattery to his or her business rather than consent being given for a new, exclusive cattery in the same area.

Cats may have considerable difficulty in settling happily into a boarding establishment, more so if they are disturbed by the high noise level of confined dogs; their diet needs careful thought and management, and their health needs constant monitoring despite the fact that all immunisation papers are in order. Cat care can be time-consuming in the extreme; they are not a get-rich-quick proposition in the boarding context. The knowledge and expertise of the proprietor are more important, and in some cases, less than ideal circumstances are partially outweighed by the high standard of personal care and understanding of cats.

It is because so many boarding kennels accept cats that both dogs and cats are referred to in this book. However, it is strongly advised that people interested in boarding cats, either in a separate cattery or in a mixed kennel, should also study the explicit information on boarding kennel construction and management which is published by the Feline Advisory Bureau and the Model Licence Conditions for catteries (FAB was a member of the working party that drew them up). The FAB also arranges courses for people who would like to run a cattery, and for young people who wish to work with animals and cats in particular.

Details of FAB publications concerning cattery construction and management, and the training schemes, may be obtained from The Boarding Cattery Officer, Feline Advisory Bureau, Taeselbury, High Street, Tisbury, Wiltshire SP3 6LD (tel: 01747 871872, www.fabcats.org).

TAKING RESPONSIBILITY FOR ANIMALS

Consider carefully the moral and ethical principles of running your own boarding kennels. You will be assuming the full responsibility for other people's animals, their cherished pets: do you know enough about animals? Loving animals, or thinking you do, and liking a country life are insufficient motives in themselves: they need to be accompanied by training, experience, dedication, discipline and a flair for dealing with people as well as with dogs and cats. Until very recently there was no law under which you had to prove that you were competent to manage a boarding kennel although the Model Licence Conditions emphasise training and there remain the 'minimum standards' for the care of animals in kennels under the 1963 Act. However, although not specifically targeted at kennels, the Animal Welfare Act (2007) brings in a 'duty of care' on all those involved with looking after animals whether they are their own pets or those belonging to other people – and it does not matter whether they are professionals and therefore paid for the service or looking after the animals for friends. This is bringing in a whole new dimension to the complexities of animal welfare in the UK, which are referred to in the appropriate chapters, but will repay careful study as the RSPCA and local authorities are already making use of the legislation.

This makes it even more important that you prepare yourself as much as possible and examine your personal motives as well as your financial resources before you take the plunge. There are many people who think they would like to run boarding kennels; making a success of running your own boarding establishment is more likely to be a long-term proposition than an overnight accomplishment.

2 Finding Your Property

It is a natural instinct to start looking at possible properties before considering the finer details of financing. Until you know what is available and have a definite proposition in mind, monetary advice on purchasing is theoretical. However, it is wise to consider how much your maximum investment should be while retaining a certain flexibility of outlook.

Having decided that a boarding kennel is what you want, the next consideration is whether the kennel is to be the sole means of support for you and your family, or whether it is intended to be profitable in its own right but not the only source of family income. A third point needs to be mentioned here; usually kennel properties are sold after the main boarding season, and as every new owner faces the possibility that some alterations will be necessary at the time of takeover, the initial outgoings will race ahead of initial income from the boarding business. Therefore, an additional income may be not only desirable but also necessary at first.

LOCATION

It follows that if either you or your partner must retain present employment, the area in which you conduct your search for a suitable property is restricted. If you are not restricted to a particular area, the choice of suitable properties countrywide will show a variation in prices. Land values, the governing factor, are much higher in the home counties and the southeast of England; however, there are thriving boarding businesses in all parts of the British Isles and clients are often prepared to travel many miles to board their pets in a kennel they know and trust. Perhaps you would like a complete change of scenery and look for a business in a part of the country which is completely new to you.

Many kennels are situated on the periphery of urban areas, while others are deep in the heart of the country. The main considerations are, first, that your kennel is in a position to attract business and, second, that it is accessible to your clients.

If the idea of a country property, cut off from civilisation, appeals to you, think whether your clients and friends will be able to find you. Even in these days of satellite navigation, directions are still important and the complicated directions such as one sometimes receives, 'A mile past the second pub on the right, down the hill and sharp left between a letterbox and a blasted oak, through the fruit farm and continue' etc are not only more than many clients can cope with but will certainly have no appeal for drivers of delivery trucks who have had enough of finding impossible places and getting stuck in narrow lanes. Your circle of personal friends might dwindle too, but on the other hand, some thriving businesses exist in such places; perhaps it depends on whether you have a country mind or are ingrained in city ways. A lot may depend on properly signposted directions to the kennel and if signs have to be posted on land which is not your own, permission has to be obtained: a point on which the local authority should be consulted.

The boarding kennel business which is situated within easy distance of a fair-sized town, positioned on a well-used A or B class road and easily approached despite traffic conditions, is the choice of many. It allows your kennel sign to be on view to passers-by who may remember it when holiday time comes around and it helps you to be found by people unfamiliar with the neighbourhood and provides easy access for deliveries. Countering an out-of-the-way position with a collection and delivery service for clients not only takes time and petrol but may not suit everybody: pet owners should always see the kennels at which they are boarding their dogs and cats. The kennel tucked away in the country is likely to be a long way from the veterinary surgeon too, and when attention is needed for a boarder it may mean a visit by the vet, not taking the boarder to the surgery.

If you employ staff, accessibility is important for them. In the winter, snowploughs clear the main roads first; country lanes, particularly those designated as parish by-roads, come last on the council's list. If you find the ideal kennel in a position which might not be a ready-made business location, it is up to you to use your ingenuity to make it a worthwhile business proposition.

Another factor which may help you decide in what area(s) your search for a suitable kennel property might be concentrated is that some areas are already well supplied with small animal boarding establishments and others are short of these facilities. Shortages can be caused by the lack of suitable property or perhaps a rather inflexible attitude towards dog boarding and catteries by an unsympathetic local authority. It may be that there is little business in the area or that hitherto nobody has been prepared to offer such a service, in which case there might be a chance for you. Whatever the area, it is a good plan to check the number of kennels with the Environmental Health Department of the local authority, do a Google search and check the dog boarding section of the Yellow Pages, which will also cover surrounding areas. In the absence of a national register of boarding kennels it is perhaps fortunate that areas covered by telephone directories are larger than those covered by councils, and most boarding kennels advertise in the Yellow Pages.

In boarding establishments everything seems to happen at once! The busiest season – the summer months – coincides with the grass growing rapidly and the weeds flourishing. The property which looks unkempt is unattractive to clients who are impressed by pleasantly situated properties. Unless you are also a dedicated horticulturist, easy landscape upkeep is a priority.

There are some very successful boarding kennels on the periphery of seaside towns. Summer boarding is augmented by holidaymakers dropping off their pets on the way, and in the winter they have plenty of clients as those involved in the holiday industry try to take their holidays.

BOARDING CAPACITY

Another important question is whether or not you are sure how many boarders you can handle, and how much boarding accommodation is needed for the concern to be profitable as a sole business interest. It is generally accepted that a husband and wife, or two business partners, would have plenty to occupy them in a kennel with a boarding capacity of 50 dogs and maybe 15 to 20 cats if they intended to do all the work themselves. Such work includes, of course, all the general maintenance as well as the care of the animals. Kennels which, from preference or lack of demand, do not board cats may have a higher dog boarding capacity.

People wishing to specialise in a boarding cattery will find that approximately 45 cats are sufficient for a couple to handle without outside assistance. Immediately staff are employed, wages become a consideration and many kennels find that part-time help at the busiest times is all they require. Certainly, new boarding kennel owners need to think very carefully about the number of boarders to which they can give the very best care, as some dogs and cats may require far more attention than others and the kennel owner should know each animal individually. However, only at the height of the boarding season are all the kennels likely to be occupied.

QUARANTINE KENNELS

There is another class of kennel purchaser: the person who wishes to buy a quarantine kennel. While many of the previously mentioned considerations apply to quarantine kennels, they are international businesses and are usually sought by people with considerable experience of caring for animals in confined environments, staff management and business organisation. There are far fewer opportunities in this sector since the introduction of the Pet Travel scheme and many quarantine kennels have closed or converted to boarding kennels in the past few years, but quarantine is likely to be a requirement of the UK for many years to come and those that remain will attract plenty of business. Quarantine kennel businesses are referred to more fully in Chapter 12.

STARTING A NEW BUSINESS

One more fact to note before you begin your search for a property is that it is usually easier to buy a licensed boarding kennel than to start from scratch at a property you already own, or one on which you already have your eye as an ideal place for a kennel business. The operative word is 'business'. Whether you intend eventually to have a large business with many kennel blocks, or a relatively small boarding concern which is not even intended to provide the sole family income, your kennel is a business and you will need a change of use permit to operate at a property which has hitherto been wholly domestic, or which may be a smallholding with either agricultural or horticultural leanings. Boarding kennels do not come under the heading of either agricultural or horticultural pursuits just because the majority of them are situated in rural or semi-rural areas.

Planning permission is needed from the local authority before a change from domestic to business use is possible. It is not only the Planning Department of the District Council which has a say in this matter. The Environmental Health (or Services) Department may make recommendations and the local Parish Council may perhaps be the most important body in some ways as its opinion, voiced to the local Council Planning Committee Meeting, may be the deciding factor for or against.

The Parish Council and the Environmental Health Officer bear the brunt of neighbourhood complaints about noise. If a new licence to board dogs is granted it may be conditional in the first instance. Too many complaints, and it might not be renewed after a period of three years, in which case it could be impossible to sell the property as a boarding kennel should the owners decide to move. Sometimes, but not always, it is easier to obtain permission for a cattery as the noise problem is minimal, but again, do not bank on sanction from the Parish Council. Reasons such as the alleged spoiling of an area of outstanding natural beauty, increase in traffic and the change of use not being necessary for horticultural or agricultural reasons could and probably will be put forward against your proposal.

If you are determined to start from scratch, contact the local Planning Department *first* to assess what chance of success you might have. Second, consult the Chief Environmental Health Officer of the district for an opinion on whether your present property, or one you are considering, might be thought suitable for small animal boarding purposes, and third, do *not* buy a property without written proof that planning consent would be granted. It would be easier to start with a licensed property, even if it were far removed from the your ideal, and concentrate on improving it to the standard you require, although the licence itself has a value that will increase the price over and above the value of the property and the current level of business. It is not impossible to obtain permission to start a new boarding kennel business from what was originally a domestic, agriculturally based or small holding residence, but the difficulties are considerable. Local authorities are more likely to look kindly on a request for permission to enlarge a small licensed kennel, provided the need can be shown, than to allow another new business in the area.

BUYING AN EXISTING BUSINESS

With a fair idea of the size and type of kennel property you require, and remembering to be flexible, what next? See as many properties as possible, which will be time-consuming and may involve many miles of travelling. The major agencies handling sales of kennel properties advertise regularly in the weekly papers *Our Dogs* and *Dog World*, in the monthly magazine *Kennel and Cattery Management* (see Appendix for addresses) and on their websites. Local estate agents also handle kennel properties occasionally. You may also consider placing an advertisement in the classified section of *Our Dogs* and *Dog World* stating that you are seeking a kennel property.

Having received details of properties which you would like to view, check that they are still available before making a long journey. A telephone call in advance could also reassure you that you really want to see the property, or ascertain that it has some drawback which would be too difficult for you to overcome. In comparison with other businesses, there are relatively few licensed kennels offered for sale at any one time; look not only at the present situation but at future possibilities. Make a list of your essentials and realise that no property will have everything right.

On arriving in the area, pop into the nearest local shop (there is usually a general store not too far away) and ask the shopkeeper if there are any good boarding kennels for dogs and cats in the area. The reply could provide you with vital information.

When you start viewing kennel properties, what should you look for? In theory, kennels should all offer a high standard of care. The new Model Licence Conditions and Environmental Health Officers increasing awareness of their responsibilities as towards animal premises have led to a considerable improvement in premises since the first edition of this book was published in 1985. However, it has to be said that many authorities do not take their responsibilities seriously enough in the animal care sector and so many of the comments hereunder remain valid.

On the other hand, the thoughtful comment by Christopher Armstrong in the Foreword needs to be emphasised here. The general public is much more aware of animal welfare than it was even 10 years ago. The television programmes on training and rescue have had an amazing impact and, as Christopher says, improvements in animal welfare are 'being driven more by customer expectation than by regulation'. There is a 'knock on' effect here, which will be discussed in later chapters, which is affecting the government's approach to licensing and regulation via the Department of the Environment, Food and Rural Affairs (Defra).

Smell

The first thing you may notice about any property you visit is either the smell, or the fact that there is no unpleasant odour about the place. Kennels do not have to smell awful; good husbandry and proper disinfection will keep the property sweet and clean despite the fact that animals are not toilet trained. A property which stinks is one to cross off your list as the basic hygiene is obviously lacking, and if accumulations of filth have been allowed to seep into unsealed wood or concrete, what other unhygienic practices are there? Could you ever rid the place of the smell, possible infection, a flea population and more bugs than you ever imagined existed? Your nose will tell you a lot, but so will the general condition of the kennels. Are they really clean? Is there any mess or uneaten food lying around? Such things attract rats, and do you want to be offering cosy boarding accommodation to all the local rodent population?

Construction

What sort of kennel construction has been used? Are the kennels purpose built or converted from other buildings? Are they built of wood, brick or breeze block? Commercial kennels are not expected to be made of wood these days. Wood may be acceptable for catteries but even this is changing as more plastic-faced building materials become available. Are the kennels inside with no attached runs? The recommendations in the Model Licence Conditions are that each kennel should have its own attached run to which the dog should have free access. Are there additional fenced exercise areas where the dogs can run free several times a day? (More on this later.) Are there safety corridors, particularly in a cattery? Is there a good secure perimeter fence to the whole property? You cannot afford escapes; some dogs can jump 6 feet with ease. Is the perimeter fence a 'jackal' fence, that is with a top section inclined inwards to the property? Is the accommodation geared to large, powerful breeds or suited only to smaller breeds? Is there a grassed exercise area? This is a necessity as some pet dogs will only urinate on grass. Are there any covered runs? These are a boon in wet weather! Bear in mind there is more than one way of setting up a workable kennel.

Is there good storage for foodstuffs, equipment and cleaning accessories? What about the boarders' food preparation area? Is the dog kitchen clean and conveniently placed?

The boarders

Look at the boarders themselves. Are they happy? They will bark at you, but note if they look cheerful. If they do not bark but just sit on their beds, consider whether they have been tranquillised. (Oh yes, it does happen!) Why? Can the present boarding kennel owner not tolerate the noise, or have the neighbours complained? Find out. It is most undesirable to tranquillise dogs unless there is a medical reason for it. Are the dogs clean, skinny, bright eyed, fat? What is your general impression? No, you are not conducting a medical examination but trying to get an idea of the care which has been given, and possibly the reputation of the business. At night, are the kennels the sort which may make the dogs feel as if they have been shut in a cupboard and forgotten, or can they see other dogs across an aisle? Remember you will be boarding pets used to living in human-sized accommodation: subjecting them to confinement in a kennel which would make a good coal bunker is not going to keep them happy and contented. Pet dogs are used to their human family connections; they are also animals that naturally live in groups if left to their own devices; they are not loners as a rule and like to be aware of the presence of companions.

Cat accommodation

Check any cat accommodation carefully. The idea that as cats are small they need minimal room is erroneous. The ideal accommodation is a single chalet for each cat, approximate measurements 1.8m × 91cm × 1.22m and with an attached run entered from a safety corridor. Chalets should be separate buildings or, if they are adjacent, a perspex sneeze barrier may be required between each run. Cat accommodation in a mixed-species kennel should be out of sight of the dogs, though it will be impossible in such circumstances to site a cattery out of earshot.

Typical Site Layout (Small)

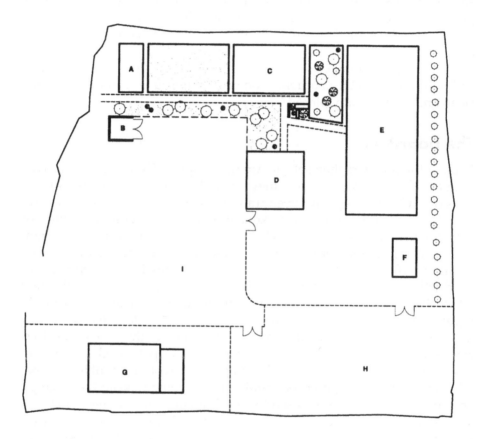

A – Isolation
B – Refuse Area
C – Cattery
D – Reception Building
E – Kennel unit (32) with central kitchen, laundry
F – Bulk Store
G – Residential Accommodation
H – Grass exercise area

Drawings courtesy of *Essential Kennel Design* by David Key

Typical Site Layout (Large)

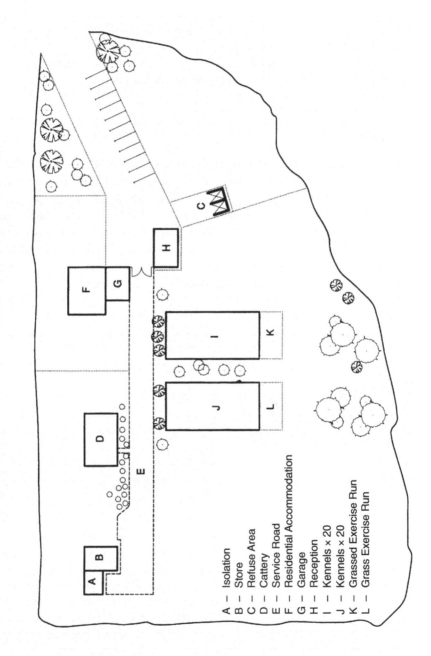

A – Isolation
B – Store
C – Refuse Area
D – Cattery
E – Service Road
F – Residential Accommodation
G – Garage
H – Reception
I – Kennels x 20
J – Kennels x 20
K – Grassed Exercise Run
L – Grass Exercise Run

Drawings courtesy of *Essential Kennel Design* by David Key

Indoor catteries may be of a 'corridor kennel' type, and each cat's compartment should be no less than the measurements given above and should lead to an exercise area of at least 1.7m². It is unfortunate that people do not realise that small cage accommodation must come as a terrible shock to the average pet cat used to a house, and that many prospective kennel owners may visit numerous establishments without seeing the ideal accommodation and therefore think that what they have seen is right.

Heating

Are the heating arrangements in both dog kennels and cat units animal proof, efficient and safe? Economy comes lower down the list than safety, but individual heating for each boarder means an overall economy when a kennel is not full, which is usually in the winter. Heating arrangements which give off fumes are best avoided for reasons of safety and efficiency. Night storage heating using cheap rate tariffs can be useful in a kennel because heating is usually only on at night when the doors are closed, so it is not wasted. Heating arrangements can be altered, or if non-existent can be installed to your requirements; allow for the expense. Note whether there are thermostatic controls on present heating arrangements as these are both economical and a great asset to the animals' comfort and well-being.

Drainage

When viewing a kennel, ask about the drainage system and the disposal of kennel rubbish. Is the dwelling house on main drainage, septic tank or cesspool drainage? Cesspools need regular emptying, and this service is becoming increasingly expensive. Does the kennel have its own septic tank? Is the disposal of kennel soil by incinerator? Is there a purpose-made incinerator? Find out. Also, never be misled by anyone who claims that a septic tank drainage system never needs maintenance. Many tanks were installed before the advent of detergents which interfere with the bacterial breakdown of the contents; modern septic tanks are usually larger than older ones which were not planned to cope with extra loads of water from automatic washing machines, for instance. Blockages sometimes occur. The council will empty tanks – for a fee – and a builder may be needed to trace and rectify a blockage. This may sound like an insurmountable problem to a town dweller who takes main drainage for granted, but country folk soon come to grips with such problems. Rural drainage systems are quite satisfactory provided you know something about the way they work and where to go for help. Anyway, you do not pay rates on septic tanks, which theoretically do not need emptying but should be periodically checked, and the council reduces its charges for regular attention.

Septic tanks and cesspools may also be emptied by private contractors. For information, consult the Yellow Pages under the heading 'Sewage Consultants'.

If you are going to construct your own kennels or you are undertaking any major renovations or rebuilding, you should obtain *Essential Kennel Design* by David Key. You can find it at Our Dogs, 1 Lund Street, Trafford Park, Manchester M16 9EJ (tel: 0870 731 6502) or go to www.ourdogs.co.uk for current price and posting charges.

BOARDING FEES AND LICENCES

Also enquire about the boarding fees currently charged. These may vary from one part of the country to another, reflecting the general local costs. However, food costs, fuel charges and mortgage rates do not alter from one region to another. It is useful to know what other kennels charge in the same area. Refer to the internet or the Yellow Pages – the local library will have copies of telephone directories – and make a few phone calls; these will provide you with the answers both to average local boarding fees and whether or not the kennels have vacancies.

Boarding licence

Find out the boarding licence renewal fee. These fees are set at the discretion of the local authority and in rural areas are generally quite reasonable. The fees are reviewed every year and are known to be higher in more urban areas. At the time of writing (2008), fees range from £80 to £350 pa. The licence is issued to the owner, not to the property; therefore, when you have found a property which you like, check with the local authority that there is no reason for a licence to be refused to a new owner, provided he or she fulfils the only personal requirement needed, namely no conviction for cruelty to animals or being banned from keeping them. Very occasionally, and for various reasons, when a boarding kennel is offered for sale the local authority may decide that the property should not be used again as a small animal boarding establishment; it may be that the licence was conditional in the first place and the premises did not really conform to the current standard or there were too many complaints from neighbours. You need to know if this is the case.

What is a neighbour? If you have always lived in a built-up area you probably consider as your neighbours those who live next door, or whose gardens adjoin your own. In a rural situation your neighbours may be quite a way from you, out of sight in fact. You may even think of a place as isolated because you cannot see another house. Unfortunately, noise carries a very long way (especially at night) when barking is not masked by other background noises or absorbed by bricks and mortar. You may find a host of neighbours appearing from nowhere as soon as you take up residence.

OWNER'S ACCOMMODATION

Naturally, it is important that the dwelling house suits your needs. Many people searching for a boarding kennel property find that if the kennels are right, the house is wrong, or vice versa. Sometimes compromises can be made, and once in a while everything will be right but, of course, these will be the most expensive properties. The priorities for the owner's accommodation are largely decided by the individual's needs, but the house should at least be tolerable as it stands because your energy will be directed to establishing your kennel business, and domestic considerations may have to take second place. Some people cannot turn a blind eye to a decor which does not suit their tastes or be happy in what they consider uncomfortable surroundings, and it is important to realise that as your kennel business will be demanding, you need to be able to relax in your home and not be depressed by it.

The location of the dwelling house in relation to the kennel buildings is something you should consider. There are boarding kennels which have the owner's accommodation very close to the dogs' quarters, and some where it is well separated. In the first instance you will have some kennels which will be handy in bad weather or for dogs needing special attention; such kennels may also be a confidence booster for the small pet which has never been away from home before and is feeling forlorn. There will also be barking in close proximity, and though this may be irritating in one way it is often a warning that something is amiss or that visitors are arriving. You soon learn to distinguish the barking for fun from the excited 'Here comes dinner' chorus and the 'What's happening now?' canine voice.

Where the kennel buildings are well separated from the owner's house it may be quieter, but there may be some very wet, cold and dark journeys to check the kennels late at night. In such kennel layouts, ensure that there is adequate outside lighting and that all kennel buildings are secure from intruders. There have been thefts of dogs from boarding kennels, and there are, unfortunately, dangers from people who either do not share our love of animals or misguidedly feel they are being ill-treated. It may be possible to install some form of alarm system – perhaps even an adaptation of a baby alarm – to alert the owner in case of need. The most sophisticated arrangement is closed-circuit television. Although this is not yet in evidence in many kennels, it is becoming more common and much less expensive as the latest cameras can be wirelessly connected to your computer.

FINANCIAL ENQUIRIES

When you have found a boarding kennel business in which you are seriously interested and intend to go forward with financial enquiries of your own, you will need to see the kennel's audited accounts. In early editions I wrote 'if they exist'. In our rapidly more regulated world there will be few kennels that can avoid having an accountant and accounts. However, some kennels, particularly those which have been considered by their owners more as a paying hobby than a fully fledged business, have no detailed accounts. A great deal of the trade will probably have been on a cash basis and the turnover nowhere near the VAT bracket. There is often a tendency to keep a kennel ticking over gently as owners cut down their workload for one reason or another because the kennel is also their home. In such cases look at the business potential; if you can acquire such a property for a reasonable price and build it up again businesswise, you may have a bargain.

Beware of the proprietor who assures you of the substantial 'cash in hand' income that is not shown in the books. There may be some, but if it is not written down it cannot be considered as part of the asking price. Financial matters are discussed in more detail in Chapter 4.

3 Professional and Other Advice

Although the boarding kennel owner's business is the care and wellbeing of other people's pet animals, it is equally important that basic business practices are understood, as profitability is necessary for the owner to be able to give the service intended. There seems to be an unfortunate element in society which intimates that it is not quite acceptable to make money out of boarding pet animals, but the boarding kennel owner is providing a valuable service and deserves to have a reasonable standard of living. Furthermore, maintaining a quality service and a professional approach to animal care cannot be done 'on the cheap'. Most kennels undercharge. The cost of pet sitting and home boarding (see Chapter 13) is often very much greater, whereas the capital and running costs are very much less.

PROPERTY

The prospective owner who is buying a kennel which already has a licence will probably need to borrow money to complete the purchase and is likely to run into the first problem when it is found that the purchase falls into two categories: a dwelling house and a business plus land. A mortgage may be available on the dwelling house but not on the business and therefore financial help will have to be procured from another source. Money must also be available to keep the kennel in operation from the time of the takeover, as foodstuffs will have to be bought in advance and clients do not pay dogs' hotel bills until they collect them. Obviously no dog departs from your kennel until its holiday has been paid for! In many cases a deposit or booking fee is payable in advance and this is not returnable in case of cancellation, but advance booking fees are not enough to keep the kennel running and suppliers of animal foods usually prefer to work on a cash with order or cash on delivery basis.

The potential kennel owner who already owns a house, has been granted a permit for a change of use from domestic to business purposes, and intends to build boarding kennels there, having obtained planning permission too of course, may also need financial assistance. Apart from the actual building of the kennels, the initial start-up and advertising costs will have to be covered. Every case is highly individual and advice needs to be tailored to a particular situation. Building societies are, as a rule, interested in private house purchases rather than business property, although, especially if you have been saving with one, it is worth asking them for a loan, for the financial climate in the 21st century is very different from that of a few years ago.

RAISING FINANCE

The cheapest money with which to finance a new business is your own – personal savings, your share portfolio if you have one, and other realisable assets such as jewellery and antiques; if you need to borrow, obtain only what you need and when you need it.

Loans

Private loans from friends or relatives may take the form of their guaranteeing a bank overdraft, or a formal loan, the terms of which should be drawn up by a solicitor. It should be made clear that such a loan does not include any control of the business.

Banks need to establish that you are a good risk before they will lend you money for a business; the manager will need to see a business plan which shows the estimated setting-up costs, the overheads or fixed costs, and the variable costs.

The setting-up costs cover professional fees, the property and initial equipment purchases, initial repairs and decoration. The fixed costs are those which you pay whether business is coming in or not: rent (there are some kennels available for rent) or mortgage repayment, rates, interest charges, telephone, power, insurance, running a car, and paying yourself a salary. The variable, or running, costs include pets' food, vets' bills (if not covered by insurance) and wages to staff. To pay the overheads and running costs, you need working capital, so you should not use all your own money on setting up; lenders are more willing to invest in tangible assets. Banks want to be helpful because they will make a great deal from you if you are successful, but they, and other lenders, are hard taskmasters if you fail.

The Small Firms Guarantee Scheme guarantees 75 per cent of a loan made by a bank up to a loan limit of £100,000 (up to £250,000 for established businesses) when the business proposition is basically sound but the borrower cannot put up enough money. A premium of 2 per cent of the amount outstanding quarterly in advance is payable to the government. For full details contact your bank or go to www.businesslink. gov.uk.

Your business plan, which will help to crystallise your own thoughts as well as persuade the bank to lend you money, should include:

- Name and address of proposed proprietor.
- Details of proposed business venture and its location.
- Information about the proprietor(s); a curriculum vitae with evidence of your ability to run the business.
- Premises. Full information, including present use, and whether planning permission is necessary for your business.
- The market research you have done on the demand for such a business in the area.
- Your financial requirements for the setting up, showing how much money is coming from which sources.
- Information on the service you plan to offer at the start and after a year.
- Staff. Whether your partner or the family will suffice, or what staff you will need to employ (full or part time).
- Budgeted expenses for the first and second years.
- Cash flow forecast for the budget periods.
- Personal and financial references.

This is a formidable list of requirements but every element is important. There are excellent computer programs available for developing business plans, but most assume that the business you want to go in for is a small service company or retail outlet, so a lot of the questions do not quite fit with your requirements. The same applies to pre-printed paper-based procedures. Most banks will provide you with such a procedure containing the documentation and structure of your proposed business plan set out in the way they want to receive it. These are all useful but you will probably find that the specifics of your proposal will need a bespoke solution. However, take careful note of the 'structure' required by each organisation (bank or building society) because you are likely to have a more sympathetic hearing if the lender is familiar with the way in which the proposal is presented. This generates more work because you may have to revise the plan for each presentation, but it is worth it.

Take detailed schedules along with you to show the bank manager when you make an appointment.

BUSINESS STRUCTURE

However you start your business, you must decide whether you intend to be a sole trader, to form a partnership or to trade as a limited company.

As a *sole trader* you will be entering the simplest form of business management and, apart from disclosing information connected with ownership of the business as required in the Companies Act 1985 if you are trading under a name other than your own, there are no other formalities. HM Revenue & Customs (HMRC) and the Department for Work and Pensions should be informed as soon as you start trading. You become self-employed, and are liable for all the debts but collect all the profits.

A *partnership* has two or more proprietors. All may share any profits, and each partner is equally responsible for all the firm's debts. A properly drawn up partnership agreement is essential as, should things go wrong, as they often do, it can be extremely difficult to settle affairs. Many partnerships go wrong because disputes and disagreements which occur had not been allowed for when setting up the partnership. Never enter into any agreement with a short-time acquaintance; never sign anything except a formal deed of partnership drawn up by a solicitor. Often it is a tragedy which brings disaster to a partnership, such as the death of a partner, or a partner's divorce proceedings; such events may terminate a business enterprise too. Tax assessments are issued in the name of the partnership, but if one partner fails to pay his or her share of the liability, the others have to pay it all. Partnerships can work but they can also be the source of many problems.

Under a normal partnership arrangement the partners are personally responsible for all the debts. The law also allows for limited liability partnerships (LLPs), which offer protection to the partners similar to that offered by a limited company but without as much red tape.

Sole traders and partnerships pay Schedule D tax: income from trades, professions or vocations. They can set against profits legitimate business expenses such as the running costs of the business, wages and salaries paid to employees, insurance, some legal and professional fees, and the cost of goods bought for resale.

A *limited company* is a legal entity in its own right, and few kennel owners operate in this way mainly because the value of the property is an integral part of the business. Furthermore, there is usually a good deal more red tape involved in running a limited company.

Whether you buy a company 'off the shelf' from a registration agent or set up one yourself, professional advice from a solicitor is essential. The objects of the company are set out in the Memorandum and Articles of Association. Limited companies are obliged by law to keep accounts to a prescribed formula, have them audited, and submit a set annually to Companies House. On small businesses, corporation tax at the time of writing is 20 per cent on profits up to £300,000 per annum, payable nine months from the end of the accounting period. There are complicated relief structures in place in respect of, for instance, capital allowances; your lawyer will advise. The period over which trading losses can be carried back and set against profits has been extended from one to three years. Business expenses that can be claimed against profits are similar to those for sole traders and partnerships.

FREE ADVICE

Business Link has been set up by the government to provide a free consultation service for small businesses. It has taken on the role of the old Training and Enterprise Councils (TECs), now absorbed into the Learning and Skills Council (LSC), and still works closely with local LSCs. The LSCs now concentrate on training, and kennel owners will find them helpful if they decide to take on young staff or require adult 'on the job' training. Further details and advice can be found in Chapter 9.

Business Link has an extensive website at www.businesslink.gov.uk that provides a wide range of direct advice on all aspects of setting up a business. The site can direct owners of small businesses towards grants as well as advice and it is worth spending some time exploring the options that are available. Throughout the UK there is a network of local operators who deliver advice and support services to people wanting to set up a new business or those wanting to grow their existing business. The network includes the Business Link operators themselves and provides links to various affiliated services. By selecting the relevant region you can immediately find a list of the local operators. Many Business Links work through local Chambers of Commerce but most are government funded companies in their own right. They can provide free advice to new businesses as well as to established ones. Owners of small businesses can sometimes get several hours of advice from an experienced businessperson who, although he or she may never have set foot in a boarding kennels, can provide ideas and local contacts as well as advising on the development of business plans. There is also a Business Link helpline (0845 600 9006).

Some assistance and advice may also be available through RuralNet and through the Rural Development programmes set up by the Department of the Environment, Food and Rural Affairs (Defra), www.defra.gov.uk. Again, the web is the quickest way to find out what is available, but those not yet connected can call 08459 335577 for more information.

It will also be helpful to browse www.connexions-direct.com. This is the government's organisation incorporating the area of youth employment and careers advice. The site is designed to support and help young people to come to what are described as 'life' decisions but there is also a network of local offices which can be helpful if you want to employ and train your own young staff. The organisation also has a budget for training.

Scotland and Northern Ireland have their own development schemes, some of which are rather more generous than those in England and Wales. Links are provided from the above sites direct to the regions.

Businesses do not pay tax on their profits until almost a year after the end of the financial year (though this does not apply to National Insurance contributions or the employer's contribution towards employees' income tax). It is important that you make provision for paying tax in your financial planning. HMRC are seldom sympathetic if you have not got the money.

SOLICITOR

Your solicitor is probably the person to give you the most important advice of all. No purchase of property should be attempted without a legal consultation, and no partnership entered into without a legal agreement drawn up by your solicitor. No papers should be signed without careful reading on your part, and all Ordnance Survey maps of the property should be checked to see that the boundaries shown are correct.

When you have decided on a property and have investigated the financial details, and have been reassured by the local authority in writing that the boarding licence will be re-issued in your name, your solicitor will handle the legal matters and make the necessary land searches. As most kennels are situated in rural or semi-rural areas, your solicitor should check whether permission has been granted, or application made, for any change of use of adjoining land though it be agricultural at the present time. The construction of new roads, a bypass or motorway, for example, may be beneficial in the long run. However, should a neighbouring farmer have been granted permission to site an intensive pig or poultry rearing unit in a field adjoining your kennel or cattery, it may be a distinct disadvantage to you. In the case of future applications you should receive notification, on which you may take action; should you not be aware that permission has already been granted, your position may be threatened. Rural areas are not always as passive as they seem at first sight and some agricultural pursuits can be smelly and noisy, and attract flies and rodents which would spread to your property.

As the defence of the 'green belt' is eroded, a major problem which has affected some established boarding kennels in recent years is the encroachment by new property developments on what was previously open country, thus bringing human habitation closer to the kennels. New residents tend to complain about noise, justifiable or not, and you may find yourself in need of legal advice. Unfortunately, the fact that you were there first is no defence. Of course you should do your best to keep aware of proposed new housing developments, which are usually a prominent subject in local newspapers, and it could be to your advantage to grasp the nettle and suggest to the developers that they may like to mention your excellent services in their promotional literature which describes the amenities of the area.

The cost of professional advice could be far less than any costs incurred through not taking it, and, as noted above, a great deal of professional advice may actually be free!

INSURANCE

You will need professional advice on insurance. Apart from the obvious fire, theft, storm damage and accidental injury policies, kennels need insurance which covers the owner and staff. You should also consider insuring the boarders while they are in the kennels or in transit between home and kennels. Insurance is available to cover escape from your premises, reimbursement of fees for you in certain cases, and payment of veterinary fees incurred while the animal is in your care. There is no greater misery than a client finding his pet has escaped and been lost, or has been stolen from your kennels: reimbursement from the insurance company may help. Your business suffers a setback when a client returns to find an ailing dog and a vet's bill a mile long.

It is not enough for an owner to agree that, should veterinary care be needed for the pet while it is in your kennel, you are empowered to call a veterinary surgeon to visit the animal. The vet's bill has to be paid, and bearing in mind the fact that many illnesses occur in what are generally termed 'unsocial hours', or at weekends, bank holidays and such times, and that the vet may have to visit the kennels, the fees are sure to be considerable. If, on the other hand, health problems have arisen with a boarder but you can meet your client with the news that the pet has been treated and that your insurance has covered the cost of treatment, or that compensation is payable in some circumstances, though it cannot prevent some sorrow it can obviate hard feelings.

Pet Plan Insurance Ltd among others specialises in boarding kennel insurance. Contact this firm and consult its representatives for an expert assessment of your own particular situation. You will find that for a relatively small sum per day, which could be added to your boarding fees without making them exorbitant, your boarders can be completely covered by insurance and you are freed from any worries in this respect. Proper insurance not only protects the dogs and their owners, it also protects your reputation.

In a physically demanding business, accidental injury is more than a remote possibility. You should consider that, if you were even temporarily disabled, it might be necessary to pay someone to do your work.

Brooks Braithwaite (Sussex) Ltd
Full page colour

Brooks Braithwaite (Sussex) Ltd
Full page edit

Insurance coverage (what are called 'key man' policies) can help in such situations. If your staff are self-employed or casual workers it would be wise to talk to them about personal accident insurance too.

In the kennel business there are a few grey areas on which it is impossible to give definitive advice. Insurance against being sued is also worth discussion.

You may wish to consult an insurance broker. The British Insurance and Investment Brokers Association (tel: 0901 814 0015, www.biba.org.uk) can send you a list of insurance brokers in your area and the Pet Care Trust holds a list of specialist insurers and provides some personal legal indemnity cover as part of its membeship fee.

ACCOUNTING

You may already have an accountant. If not, or perhaps because you are moving into an entirely new area, you may wish to ask for advice on accountancy firms from a local bank manager. Your accountant will advise you what he or she requires to complete your accounts in a way that will satisfy HMRC. To ensure this it will be necessary to keep careful books, though you may have found during your search for a boarding kennel that many owners could not produce either satisfactory summaries of income and expenditure or audited accounts, or that some accounts which were produced were incomprehensible. Kennels are indeed busy places in which the boarders come first and everything else takes second place; when the day's physical work is done it is too easy to put off the bookwork. That is not the road to profitability. A good accountant (as distinct from one who just puts the figures together at the end of the year) can make an enormous difference to your long-term future. Advice on investments, pensions and improvements to the kennels and to your home should always be run past your accountant first, for there are many ways in which a 'switched on' accountant can save and make you money.

LOCAL OFFICIALS AND WELFARE OFFICERS AND REPRESENTATIVES

It is essential to contact the local authority to discuss with them any matters concerning the continued approval of the kennel as a boarding establishment, or the possibility of enlarging it. Many departments will have views and recommendations on boarding kennels, but the council's Environmental Health Department approves the site, the buildings, the drainage and waste disposal with a view to health matters and noise pollution. Complaints of undue noise, or any noise at all in some instances, are made to the Environmental Health Officer, who will investigate them. In contrast, council officials are probably not aware of the best ways to handle your boarders' day-to-day needs; they are concerned with the suitability of the property from their point of view, not necessarily from yours. Neither is the council interested in your personal suitability, training, or experience with animals other than the fact that you have not been convicted for cruelty to animals. You should take this opportunity to discuss the licence conditions of the premises (there are bound to be some), for they and any changes envisaged must be taken into account when you are estimating your outgoings (see Chapter 4).

Complaints of cruelty, or alleged cruelty, are almost always made direct to the RSPCA and it is useful to contact your local RSPCA inspector in your early days of kennel ownership as you may be asked to assist this organisation at times by temporarily housing a dog or cat. While you should be aware that the RSPCA, unlike the officers of the local authority, do not have any right of entry to your property, and would have to produce a police warrant to gain admittance against your wishes, it is wise to build a good rapport with them and to instil confidence in your ability and business.

There were concerns when the Animal Welfare Act (2007) was being debated that the RSPCA or other organisations might be given extended powers. This has not proved to be the case and any 'official' approach to enter your premises by anyone other than an Environmental Services Officer (or someone who has been authorised by the licensing officer and of whom you have previously been notified) or a policeman with a warrant should be resisted. This is important. As I write, the RSPCA have brought several cases against kennels for failing in their duty of care. So far these have all failed because the courts have realised that the Society had been 'rehearsing' witnesses – clearly a matter of contempt. Furthermore, the matters being complained of which I have been notified about have been minor and subjective so would probably not have been proven anyway. Such cases are sometimes brought to the court as a part of a lobby group's or charity's publicity campaign and sometimes by over-enthusiastic local employees of such societies who believe they have 'right' on their side.

These matters are discussed in more detail in Chapter 5.

As kennel owners are always advised to insist that all boarders should have current immunisation certificates, it does not make sense to accept a rescued animal which has no health records. If you have no accommodation for such animals, you must make it clear that you cannot accept them. Even if your kennel has a separate isolation unit which could be used in such circumstances, you are not obliged by law to take in such animals with their possible health risks, and your paying clients do not deserve to have their pets endangered. It is best to discuss such matters fully with your local police and RSPCA so that they are aware of your decision and whether or not you can help in exceptional circumstances. These organisations should be fellow professionals and you all deserve to know the policies and not be forced into last-minute decisions which may be based solely on emotive reasons. The difference between you and these other bodies is that you are self-employed and cannot afford to take risks which might be detrimental to your business, while they are funded.

That being said, as of 1 April 2008 the current responsibility of the police for stray dogs, which they have shared with local authorities since 1992, has ended and local authorities are now entirely responsible. Many authorities have already developed good relationships with local kennels to house strays on a regular basis and have been prepared to give planning permission for suitable facilities to be constructed at a suitable distance from the commercial facility.

These arrangements have generally worked well and such kennels have also been used by other rescue organisations when necessary. The lesson to be learned is that, as a business, you must be ready to recognise new opportunities when they arise and change your procedures and sometimes your premises to take advantage of those altered circumstances. We will return to this and related matters in Chapters 10 and 12.

Police dogs, that is, those owned by the force and not strays, are another matter. Occasionally accommodation is needed for these dogs, which are healthy and fully inoculated. This is a different matter entirely and subject to special negotiation.

When you take over another person's business, the ideal arrangement is to take over the kennels empty and arrange for a thorough cleaning and disinfection before your customers arrive. In practice this may not work and you may find yourself taking over a kennel in mid-season or with some boarders in residence even though the summer rush is over. You will undoubtedly be glad of their boarding fees anyway, but it would be a good plan to rotate the accommodation so that you can have a thorough cleansing and disinfecting job done by a specialist professional firm. Your residents can then be changed over to the professionally disinfected buildings while the others are being treated. A cleaning and disinfecting routine as suggested by the professional organisation should ease your worries concerning proper disease control on your premises. Waiting until you have an outbreak of infection is leaving it too late.

The Department for Environment, Food and Rural Affairs (Defra) may also be consulted either at their head office or through the local Divisional Veterinary Officer at a Defra area office. See www.defra.gov.uk or telephone 08459 335577.

4 Finance and Running Costs

The estimation of running costs for a boarding kennel business during the first year of ownership is not an easy task. Hopefully, you will have seen your predecessor's audited accounts, but even so your running costs may bear no relation to those. In the first place, all costs are sure to have risen and second, your priorities may not have been the same as those of the previous owner. The other, perhaps the most important, factor is that you do not know how much business you will be doing. Perhaps your predecessor has allowed the business to lapse, and while you have been able to purchase it at an advantageous price, estimating how much and how soon you can build it up may be impossible to forecast with any accuracy.

INCOME

Boarders' fees will probably provide most of your income when you start up. Reckon on being full a third of the year and allow, say, £8.50 to £15.00 per dog per day (the actual amount will depend on your geographical location and the quality of the kennel), divide the resulting figure by 3 and multiply the answer by 365 to give you the worst picture. Your objective should be to work towards a 55 per cent occupancy, but more of this later. Any other sales of goods, accommodation or services (see Chapter 13) will bring in more. It is clear that an additional income from outside the business is often essential during the early stages.

If a married couple are running the business together, the wife could be paid the equivalent of the personal allowance before paying income tax, but these things change and your accountant should ensure you pay the minimum tax.

OUTGOINGS

Some expenses will be the same whether you are doing business or not. These fixed costs include rent, mortgage or loan repayments. These can be estimated with fair accuracy, barring fluctuations in interest rates, and can be paid monthly. Many bills – gas, electricity, telephone and some water authority charges – may also be paid on a monthly basis. This can ease the shock of a sheaf of bills arriving at the same time, and in the case of varying accounts such as electricity, gas and telephone you will receive statements which will show you how your payments are matching up with your debts. Heating and lighting charges can be estimated by the companies concerned, and may or may not work out exactly at the end of the year.

The licence renewal fee must be thought of, but these fees are reviewed each year and vary in different parts of the country. There may be some extra expense for the periodic draining of septic tanks, but the local council or sewerage disposal service usually has a set rate for this and reduces the charge for regular attention. However, any unblocking must be contracted for separately with a private contractor; allow for this.

Depending on what disposal system you have at your kennel, and what refuse collecting services are offered by the local council under your council tax, you may find that you have to pay extra for the collection of garbage which may come under the heading of trade waste rather than domestic refuse. Question this in advance for, as in the case of a non-functioning septic tank, a kennel waste problem needs sorting out immediately, not tomorrow or next week. If this is a situation you have to deal with on an extra payment basis, allow for it, as it will be a continuing problem.

Another expense will be the running costs of your car or van, but make this business item pay its way by using it as an advertising medium – see that it carries the name of your kennels, the location and telephone number, and that it is clean and gives the impression of a hygienic establishment.

Though you may have made some capital investment in additions, alterations and redecoration to the dwelling house and kennels, maintenance and general upkeep of the whole property must be allowed for. Unfortunately, the boarders will probably damage their accommodation far more than you would ever have imagined. Kennels and cat units must be escape-proof. Though good-quality purpose-made kennels, and kennel gates, runs and fencing, may be expensive initially, they are likely to give fewer maintenance problems over the years. Outside exercise runs take a beating too if they are anything other than paving or concrete, and they, and other grassed parts of the property, will need mowing. Allow for the expense and upkeep of garden machinery and perhaps for some casual labour in this department, as your busiest season will coincide with rapid growth of grass and weeds. Gravel runs will need resurfacing, perhaps not frequently, but it is an expense to bear in mind.

Reference is made throughout this book to the Model Licence Conditions. The conditions themselves will be discussed in more detail later, in Chapter 5, but when you are taking on new premises it is important to realise that the local authority may impose conditions on the licence that have not been implemented under the current licence. The Model Conditions have a clause that requires the local authority to be sensible in their implementation and this has often resulted in an agreement to delay required improvements at some premises. There may be many reasons for such an arrangement but one of the most common is that the owners are close to retirement and the local Environmental Health Officer has felt that with an otherwise well-run kennel, the upheaval may be financially or socially impractical. However, this means that some major works may be required when a new owner takes over. If such works require major investment (the kennels may require new flooring, drainage or even the replacement of one or more kennel blocks), they may be spread over several years. However, the costs do need to be included in your business plan and may affect your expenses from the first year.

Two further items of major importance are food for the boarders and cleaning materials, including disinfectants. Methods of feeding dogs and cats in the kennel environment are discussed in Chapter 7.

Cleaning materials and disinfectants are another large item in the kennel budget. Chapter 6 deals with disinfectants in some detail; remember that the cheapest are not necessarily the most effective and that disinfection is a vital part of the daily kennel routine.

Stationery and postage costs arise as they will in any business and you should allow for regular local advertising plus occasional advertising farther afield.

You should, of course, remember your own National Insurance obligations. Call the National Insurance Contributions Office on 0845 302 1479 or visit www.hmrc.gov.uk/nic/ for advice, remembering that self-employed people (whether the kennel owner or staff) with small earnings may obtain exemption from payments as explained in the official leaflets available.

VALUE ADDED TAX

HM Customs and Excise is now incorporated into HMRC (along with the old Inland Revenue) and your local office will supply the necessary instruction leaflet and show you how to deal with the paperwork regarding Value Added Tax (VAT). If your annual business turnover exceeds a figure (fixed in each Budget), you must register for VAT, and your accounts will have to show details of all VAT charged to customers (the standard rate is currently 17.5 per cent). VAT returns have to be completed quarterly, and it is wise to keep VAT collected in a separate bank account, so the cash is available when you have to pay it out and not dipped into for current expenditure. On the credit side, you can claim repayment of VAT on your business purchases: animal foodstuffs, petrol, cleaning materials and so on.

It is a difficult choice for businesses close to the threshold. You can opt to register for VAT even if your turnover is beneath the threshold so that you can reclaim VAT. However, this means that your *charges* are likely to be 17.5 per cent *above* those of your competitors even though they are subject to higher expenses because they have to pay VAT on their purchases.

KEEPING ACCOUNTS

When in business on your own account, you should keep the books in a form recommended by your accountant, so he or she can present them to HMRC annually for income tax assessment and also prepare a profit and loss account for you. It is easier if the work is done regularly, and it can be very simple. These days accounts are often completed more conveniently on a computer but this is not always the most economical or convenient method, as discussed later in this and future chapters.

In the *cash book* will be recorded income (on the left-hand side of a double-page spread) and outgoings (on the right-hand side). Each transaction shows on one line the date, description of goods sold or service provided (or bought), cheque number, invoice number, cost, and VAT. The *petty cash book* records small sums paid out daily in cash. The *wages book* – if you employ staff – shows each person's gross earnings, tax deductions, NI contributions, net pay and the employer's NI contribution as well.

If you deal regularly with certain suppliers, you will find a *purchase ledger* useful, each supplier having a page or section. You are unlikely to have numerous dealings with individual customers, so a *sales ledger* will probably not be called for.

There are many pre-printed ledgers available from any stationer's. You do not have to create them yourself. And of course this can all be done on a spreadsheet on a computer.

Your accountant should be able to guide you through the maze; the more work you do, the lower the bill will be.

This is a convenient time to discuss the use of computers in kennels. Like VAT, there are advantages and disadvantages and these apply to book-keeping and to animal accommodation. As people become more computer literate (and certainly many new owners of kennels will have extensive experience of computers in their previous working life) there is a tendency to feel that no one can do without them. However, computers are designed for businesses where hundreds of transactions each day, each hour or even each second, are the norm. This is not the case in an average kennel. There are a few petty cash payments now and again, occasional weekly bills, a sheaf of monthly bills and half a dozen quarterly bills. Income usually comes from the payments by clients when they collect their pets and is in cash, by cheque or by credit card so there are very few invoices to raise. Even when a large kennel is full, 30 transactions in a day would make it a very busy one. A card index has the advantage that the cards are filled out by the client, whereas on a computerised system the details have to be input by you and, in general, turning the pages of a diary is faster than a computer search where not all the details are displayed. (Kennel accommodation programmes are dealt with in Chapter 8.)

This makes it sound as if computers are a waste of time for kennels, but this is not the case – they are very useful but you can manage without them. If you are computer literate, a simple book-keeping programme can save a lot of adding up (and can easily calculate VAT, for instance) and provide useful management information on a regular basis. But it should be recognised that the time saved may not be as great as you might imagine. Every day, every week, every month and every quarter, someone has to sit down and ensure that data is entered, money in and money out is accounted for and the calculations are made for your bank and for your accountant. This regular office work is essential if you are to run an efficient and profitable business. Whether or not you are using paper 'books' plus a calculator (one with a till role is essential for checking) or a computer-based electronic series of spreadsheets, the time must be found to complete the work. Of course, a computer may save your accountant some time too, and the greatest advantage would be to use the programme that he or she recommends (but this may be a much more complicated and expensive one than you need).

More on computers in Chapter 8, but in the meantime remember that if you do use a computer that contains records of your clients other than just their name, address and telephone number, you may have to register under the Data Protection Act of 1984. Contact the Information Commissioner's Office at www.ico.gov.uk.

GETTING THE BEST DEALS

The answer to getting the best deals is to approach manufacturers until you find a sympathetic ear! Purpose-built kennels, run fencing, kennel 'furniture and furnishings' – that is, beds and bedding – pet foods and disinfectants are made by firms specialising in products for the pet trade. Many other products, perhaps all, will have to be obtained from general suppliers, but not all suppliers are willing to sell to kennels at trade prices. Manufacturers exhibiting at the larger championship dog shows and trade exhibitions are usually helpful.

Meanwhile it remains essential for the kennel owner to ensure that running costs are kept to the minimum through his or her own individual efforts. Always ask for trade prices; you are in business and are buying for your business. Ask for discounts on bulk purchases. Check the price of pet foods from several sources – you will be surprised at the variation on individual products. Perhaps there is an agricultural trade supply centre in your area from which you can purchase certain items. When approaching bulk suppliers or cash and carry depots you must have done your homework and know which products you want to buy because these non-kennel orientated merchants will be unable to advise you on products to suit your special needs. The new kennel owner who has experience of dog or cat breeding, exhibiting, nursing or veterinary care has a head start in knowing which are the most useful and advantageous products to buy.

The kennel owner needs to purchase at advantageous prices and cannot afford the time to be constantly chasing after information. This book will give readers some leads from which to work and it is worth attending the pet trade show Pet Index, which is held at the National Exhibition Centre in Birmingham each September.

UPDATING YOUR KNOWLEDGE

In order to make the most of your business potential, it is necessary to regularly update your knowledge of the financial, commercial and animal care aspects of your kennels. Boarding kennels are essentially individual businesses but, unfortunately, that individuality leads to isolation from other businesses in the area, and from others of the same kind.

New, and intending, owners of boarding kennels are strongly advised to read either, or both, of the two weekly dog papers, *Our Dogs* and *Dog World*, which are available to order from your local newsagent, as the features 'Educational Events' and 'Chances To Learn' are published weekly therein and some of the subjects scheduled may be of interest.

Courses on various subjects are available from the Animal Care College, Index House, High Street, Ascot, Berkshire SL5 7EU (tel: 0845 123 8360; e-mail: acc@rtc-mail.org.uk; website: www.animalcarecollege.co.uk) and from the College of Animal Welfare, www.caw.ac.uk, or Wood Green Animal Shelters, Godmanchester www.woodgreen.org.uk (tel: 0780 062 1122). Subjects such as animal first aid, feline behaviour, and kennel and cattery management are among those offered.

It may also be useful to attend some of the lectures which are given occasionally by members of the Association of Pet Behaviour Counsellors, www.apbc.org.uk, tel: 01386 751151 and the Association of Pet Dog Trainers, www.apdt.co.uk, tel: 01285 810811. These are always advertised in the weekly canine press and it is well worth making an effort to attend some of them. Money spent on broadening your knowledge is an investment in your business.

5 Laws and Orders: Statutory Requirements

Boarding kennel owners should know which laws concern their trade and remember that not all parts of the British Isles, or all types of kennels, are subject to the same laws. However, a law which applies in one country of the United Kingdom will probably have a counterpart which applies in another.

In Northern Ireland the Northern Ireland Welfare of Animals Act (172) and Animal Boarding Establishments Regulations (NI) of 1974 apply but as discussed below, all this is changing.

THE ANIMAL WELFARE ACT 2007

The new Animal Welfare Act has now worked its way through the system and was placed on the statute book in April 2007. It brings in a 'duty of care' placed on anyone who has responsibility for an animal whether private or professional, and enables a raft of Secondary Legislation which is gradually being put in place by the Department of the Environment, Food and Rural Affairs (Defra). Initially, this work has been confined to Codes of Practice and at the time of writing (February 2008) the Dog and the Cat Codes are almost complete. Those relating to 'small and furries', exotics, fish, pet shops and boarding kennels will follow over the next few years. Incidentally, there has been a great deal of work put into these Codes. Many consulted have argued that they should be detailed (the first draft of the Dog Code ran to almost 40 A4 pages) while others, the RSPCA and myself included, felt that they should be short and to the point, arguing that there was no point in writing and distributing a document that those it was aimed at would not read. These Codes are designed to be rather like the Highway Code: not an integral element of the law but guidance which, if ignored, could provide the evidence for prosecution.

It was originally envisaged by the Act that there would be an extension of licensing which would become the Secondary Legislation as mentioned in the last paragraph. This concept is still within the Animal Welfare Act and may well be implemented but the current thinking within Defra (and I emphasise that this may change) is that the Codes of Practice might provide enough of a framework to ensure that the objectives of the Act are achieved. Defra is committed to what is referred to in government circles as 'light touch' regulation on the basis that if there is not a problem do not legislate. This may mean that the current licence system for pet shops and boarding kennels is scaled down to, say, registration. Needless to say, this is likely to be fiercely opposed by local authorities and lobby groups who will argue that the basis for the welfare of animals in confined environments is being undermined. It may not even be welcomed by proprietors who may see the possession of a licence as evidence that their premises, practices and processes achieve a satisfactory standard. In any event, the Codes for boarding kennels are not likely to be discussed until at least 2009 and it may be a year or even two before they are agreed and published.

To complicate the issue, the establishment of the Scottish Executive, the Welsh Parliament and Stormont in Northern Ireland has meant that many aspects of regulation once controlled from London have now been, or are likely to be, transferred to Edinburgh, Cardiff or Belfast. Animal welfare is one of these and I recently received a substantial document on dog care and welfare from the Scottish Parliament which had every indication that its requirements will be compulsory and have the force of law. This is not the only area in which Scotland, Wales and Ireland are moving apart from England but it is one which is seen to be relatively easy to implement and will have the effect of establishing different regimes (albeit all with the same objective) in each country.

It takes some years for changes of this nature in the law to have an effect. Unlike the banning of smoking or the use of mobile phones while driving, which are straightforward 'black and white' issues, each with a precise date from which everyone was expected to observe new rules, animal welfare is much more complicated. Some people believe that feeding a complete food is damaging to the long-term health of the dog or cat. If you feed a complete food is this a dereliction of duty? More critically, at what point do you euthanase an animal in your care? Both keeping it alive and putting it asleep might be the wrong decision in the eyes of, say, the RSPCA, your veterinary surgeon, your EHO or the owner. The recent court actions by the RSPCA have focused on not providing sufficient food or water in a kennel environment and in the case of a private pet owner, on not taking a dog to a veterinary surgeon when it had a chronic ear condition. The actions failed for technical reasons but until the courts have had more experience of such actions we will not know how the Act will finally be interpreted.

It is therefore important to tread carefully. Although I must emphasise that statistically the likelihood of any individual being affected is extremely small, it is as well to be ready.

The objectives of the Act are admirable and I believe it is a force for good in caring for animals in society but, in the meantime, there are many both on the committees and employed by charities whose views are unreasonable at best and extreme at worst. As the Act is 'enabling' legislation it does mean that private prosecutions can and will be brought. I also believe that the courts will be sensitive and sensible (as they have been so far) but advice from the Self Help Group for Farmers, Pet Owners and Others (SHG) is should be read carefully and heeded.

They say you should be prepared. If a uniformed RSPCA inspector arrives on your premises he or she may knock at the door or you might even see the inspector looking into sheds, stables and buildings. The inspector is likely to say that a report about your animals has been made and he or she would like to check them. The inspector should not be allowed to do so. He or she has no legal rights to be on your property, no special legal powers, cannot demand entry and you have no obligations to answer any of the inspector's questions. You should be polite, but very firm. Refuse entry. And tell the inspector to leave. If he or she refuses you are entitled to use reasonable force to eject the inspector, as you would any other common trespasser.

If a police officer is present, ask him or her to leave unless he or she has a warrant, or is going to arrest you. Do not volunteer any information at all and refuse to answer any questions. Do not even give your name. There have been cases where the uniform, a caution, and the general demeanour of a uniformed RSPCA inspector have been used to intimidate people – not just kennel owners. You may feel that you are being helpful if you let an inspector in to have a look round and you may feel that you have nothing to hide but do not let yourself be lulled into a false sense of security. Many innocent pet owners have lost their animals in this way and there appears to have been a rise in RSPCA private prosecutions since the Animal Welfare Act.

Make sure you ask for name, number and rank of any person present and write them down. Cancel going shopping next day: RSPCA personnel have a habit of returning when you, the proprietor, are not there and may intimidate staff. If this happens to you immediately contact your veterinary surgeon to come out and write a report and act immediately on any recommendations he or she suggests. Take photographs of all your stock, land and premises. Then get specialist legal advice and ring 0870 072 6689 or 02380 440999. The SHG know of solicitors, barristers, and specialist vets and land experts who are accepted by the courts as expert witnesses. I hope none of this will happen to you but in any case do not treat the RSPCA lightly. It is an immensely wealthy and incredibly powerful organisation which has openly admitted to breaching people's civil and legal rights on the grounds that its responsibility is to the welfare of animals. For further information go to http://the-shg.org. As Defra makes clear on its own website: 'The RSPCA cannot issue formal improvement notices under the Act. They do, and will continue to, issue their own informal "improvement notices". These are not formal notices under the Act and have no power in law.'

Finally, in case you think I am paranoid, I should say that despite these genuine concerns, the RSPCA does some useful work. Its contribution to educating the public and to pet rescue are substantial. Most of its employees are genuinely concerned to ensure that animals are looked after properly and the organisation often brings examples of genuine cruelty to the attention of the public and the courts. But as in every complex, multi-layered organisation there will inevitably be failures of management and process which can impact unfairly on individuals and businesses.

THE ANIMAL BOARDING ESTABLISHMENTS ACT 1963

This requires that dog and cat boarding kennels in England, Scotland and Wales be licensed by the district authority in which they are situated and that they shall be inspected by an officer appointed in writing by that authority. The district authority is required to specify on the licence the conditions which appear to be necessary to secure the objects of the Act.

The basic requirements of the Animal Boarding Establishments Act 1963 stipulate that dogs be kept in accommodation of suitable size and construction, temperature, ventilation, lighting and cleanliness. Boarded animals must be adequately supplied with suitable food and drink, and be visited by the kennel staff at suitable intervals. Dogs must be kept in secure accommodation, reasonable precautions are to be taken to prevent the spread of infectious diseases and appropriate steps must be taken in the event of an emergency. A suitable and consistent level of management should be maintained.

When the Act had been in force for some years it became apparent that boarding kennel conditions varied considerably in different parts of the country; some kennels were decidedly unsatisfactory and there seemed to be no uniform interpretation of the schedule of conditions or the standard of inspection.

In 1970 the British Veterinary Association (BVA) published a schedule of conditions for the use of local authorities when issuing licences under the Act, but there was still concern in some areas that boarding establishments were not altogether satisfactory. Therefore, in 1975 the BVA published a guide for district authorities and their veterinary inspectors employed under the Act. The guide was revised in 1985 and copies may be obtained from the BVA (tel: 020 7636 6541). The BVA guide is comprehensive, concise and explicit in describing the conditions under which your kennel should operate but has been superseded by the Model Licence Conditions already referred to in previous chapters.

Model Licence Conditions

The BVA recommendations of 1985 were considered inadequate by the Chartered Institute of Environmental Health (CIEH). Although they provided good advice for kennel owners and veterinary surgeons, the CIEH had not been involved with their development and they were therefore not user friendly for Environmental Health Officers (sometimes referred to as Environmental Services Officers – EHOs or ESOs). The CIEH's response was to publish its own guidelines for its members in 1993. Although its intentions were good, the document was written entirely from the perspective of the Institute and was so prescriptive and restrictive that it would have put many kennels out of business: it was immediately clear that the document would do more harm than good. It was withdrawn under pressure from the Pet Care Trust (then the Pet Trade and Industry Association), which persuaded the CIEH to form a working party with the British Small Animal Veterinary Association (BSAVA), the Feline Advisory Bureau (FAB) and the Association of District Councils (ADC) (now the Local Government Association – LGA) to work through the document and publish advice that would raise the standard of care in kennels and catteries and be a useful guide both for EHOs and kennel owners. The final document, now known as the Model Licence Conditions (MLCs), was published in 1995. It is now clearly dated and needs revision but this has been set aside in view of the work being done by the Department of the Environment, Food and Rural Affairs (Defra) as described earlier in this section. However, for the moment, the MLCs remain firmly in place.

The nature of local government requires a somewhat bureaucratic approach to legislation. As we have seen, the original 1963 Act was not specific. It demanded that animals were provided with a suitable environment to ensure that they were warm and dry and that they were kept fed, watered and clean. It also brought in the requirement for licensing and other administrative procedures that were designed to ensure that the premises were not overcrowded. These measures did improve conditions for pet animals, but despite the previous veterinary attempts over 30 years, perceptions, technology and expectations change and the MLCs were established to further interpret the 1963 Act in the light of these developments.

The foreword to the MLCs (there are two, one for kennels and one for catteries) reads, 'Animal boarding establishments fulfil a public need. The public has a right to expect that all premises satisfy basic standards relating to the health, welfare and safety of the animals boarded. Establishment owners should know the minimum standards they must attain. The licensing authority should apply the standards sensibly and appropriately.' There is sometimes considerable disagreement between the EHO and the boarding kennel owner about what is 'sensible and appropriate' (and the Pet Care Trust is often called upon to help resolve such disputes), but the paragraph remains an important mission statement for the boarding kennels and catteries industry.

Each set of conditions is divided into several sections covering all practical aspects of kennel construction and management. Each section consists of formal interpretation of the 1963 Act and accompanying notes and discussion. It is a useful document and there is no doubt that there have been significant improvements to many establishments where the MLCs have been implemented.

Of course, improvements cost money and the fees charged by pet boarding establishments have increased sharply since 1998–99 when the recommendations started to 'bite'. On the other hand, the best boarding kennels and catteries already complied, and were already more expensive. What has happened is the smaller, less animal welfare orientated, 'back pocket' kennel has been forced to improve its standards (and in some cases gone out of business) and this has to be good for the industry as a whole. Understandably, some kennel owners complain about the higher level of care they are expected to deliver. However, it must be remembered that many commercial, privately owned companies, restaurants being the prime example, have been subject to these sorts of demanding requirements for many years and have, in the long term, profited by the higher standards imposed.

There have been three main problems with the MLCs. The first is that too many EHOs are inexperienced in the requirements of animal care in confined environments and do not monitor premises effectively and/or adequately, while some EHOs sometimes try to apply the standards too rigidly. For instance, if the specified area of runs in a kennel block is 5 per cent too small, they insist that the block is totally unsuitable and cannot be used. This ignores the 'sensible and appropriate' advice of the foreword to the MLCs, for if runs are slightly too small for medium-sized dogs (the Conditions allow for two sizes of kennel), they are likely to be perfectly adequate for small/toy dogs. This is a difficulty that can only be solved by ensuring that EHOs whose knowledge and understanding of the industry is inadequate are provided with accurate information and advice. The Chartered Institute of Environmental Health is aware of the problem but local authorities' budgets are under continual pressure. The licensing of boarding kennels (and pet shops too) is a responsibility that is often added to the list of an officer whose expertise might be in food hygiene or, in one instance known to the author, the licensing of taxi cabs. The Pet Care Trust has begun to implement a programme of Continuing Professional Development (CPD) for EHOs and this is likely to improve the situation – although not for those authorities who take this area of their responsibility rather too lightly.

The second is that veterinary advice has been consistently against a 'Kennel and Exercise' regime as compared to a 'Kennel and Run' regime. K&E consists of relatively small kennels. The routine is that dogs are taken to a large exercise area several times a day to run, stretch their legs and give them a change of surroundings. This regime has the advantage that the dogs are handled regularly by the kennel staff, while the new environment enables them to exercise freely. There are, unfortunately, disadvantages too. Moving each dog several times a day and ensuring that the exercise areas remain clean is very time-consuming and the veterinary and environmental health members of the MLC working party felt that when a kennel was very busy, these exercising and cleansing routines could and would be curtailed. There were also worries about cross-infection between dogs and, perhaps, the possibility of fighting if, to save time, kennels exercised groups of dogs together and did not supervise them adequately. Consequently, the working party agreed that, subject to exercise areas being easily cleaned, the regime could be retained for existing kennels but that all 'new build' kennels should be 'Kennel and Run'. This means that each dog (or dogs if belonging to the same family and the owners' written permission has been obtained to keep them together) has a bed area and attached run that is large enough for exercise and which is permanently available to it during the day. The disadvantages of *this* regime, of course, are that first, the dog does not 'explore' the run area in the way that it does when introduced to a new one (even if it was in it an hour or two before), so, in fact, it gets less exercise. Second, it is quick and easy to clean the kennel and run, so the dogs do not have the more regular human contact that can make their days in the kennels easier and less stressful. Whichever system is used, the proprietor has the continuing responsibility of ensuring that the shortcomings of each regime are overcome by established routines that will give the dogs the best possible care.

Finally, it has to be accepted that the wide range of premises involved means that the MLCs cannot cover every eventuality and are somewhat cumbersome and restrictive. However, there is no doubt that they have improved standards of care in boarding kennels, so it is a concern that not every local authority has moved towards implementing them although most now do so. This means that in some areas, a proportion of kennels and catteries are managed and maintained without careful monitoring by the licensing authority and so still fall below the standards the public is entitled to expect.

Every boarding kennel and cattery owner should have copies of the conditions. They are available from the Chartered Institute of Environmental Health, Chadwick Court, 15 Hatfields, London SE1 8DJ (tel: 020 7928 6006).

Apparently excluded from inspection under the 1963 Act are pet shop kennels and those attached to veterinary premises which are ancillary to the main business, as these are covered by the Pet Animals Act 1951, training kennels for police or guide dogs, obedience training kennels, greyhound kennels and hunt kennels where the hounds belong to the hunt. Breeding kennels are normally covered by the Dog Breeding (Welfare) Act of 1999 but breeding kennels which are also boarding kennels may be subject to the 1963 Act also. Kennels at airports or hotels, or in other situations where the boarding of animals is not the prime occupation, are also exempt from inspection under the Act, but there is now an expectation that they should be inspected. Quarantine kennels are licensed by Defra and are inspected under Defra regulations, not under the 1963 Act, unless they also have domestic boarding sections, in which case the 1963 Act will apply to that section as would the Breeding of Dogs Act should it also be a breeding establishment.

Owners of boarding kennels should obtain a copy of the 1963 Act, not only to become familiar with the conditions which they are expected to fulfil but also to make sure that they understand their own rights. The Act instructs a local authority to pay particular regard to certain requisites before issuing a licence, but without prejudice to their discretion to withhold a licence on other grounds. In short, although a person may be eligible to hold a licence and the premises are apparently suitable to be licensed as a boarding establishment, a licence may be withheld for other reasons. This is particularly important to people who may wish to start a new kennel at a property which seems eminently suitable but for which a licence application may be refused. They are entitled to know why it has been refused or, if a complaint has been made against them, to ask who made the complaint.

Kennel inspection

Under the terms of the 1963 Act the local authority may authorise in writing any of its officers, or any veterinary surgeon or veterinary practitioner, to inspect your kennel. You may not obstruct or delay such a person and, in fact, you may come to know your local inspector very well. Despite the wording of the Act, the inspector may not be a veterinary surgeon and he or she is not obliged to have any knowledge of dogs or the animal boarding business; Environment Chief Officers, on whom falls most of the work of inspection and investigation of complaints, are not specifically trained in canine and feline knowledge, which is not intended to imply that they have no knowledge of dogs or cats at all.

No person other than the authorised officer of the district authority has any statutory right to inspect your kennels and no representative of any organisation, charitable or otherwise, has a right of entry to your property without your permission. Animal welfare societies do not have an automatic right of entry, but, of course, you may invite whom you wish to see your kennels. Make sure that you, and your staff, know who must be admitted and who should await the owner's permission to enter. There is no need to be rude or unwelcoming, but apart from the official inspector, visitors come by appointment. It is important to remember that some people may have visited other boarding establishments prior to yours and that such premises may be neither as clean nor as free from infection as your property and that you have the health of your boarders to consider. Some visitors may be quite content with a talk in your reception area; you should ascertain the purpose of their visit before deciding to show them round the premises. Visitors will be an excitement for your boarders and the dogs will enjoy a good bark. On the other hand you may prefer that they are not disturbed unnecessarily.

THE DISEASES OF ANIMALS (APPROVED DISINFECTANTS) ORDER 1978 (AMENDED 1991 AND UPDATED 2004)

This applies to quarantine kennels, which are required to use an approved disinfectant shown on the list included in the Order. However, every boarding kennel owner should have a current copy of the list, which may be downloaded from www.opsi.gov.uk/si/si2004/20042891.htm.

Copies of the above Acts (but not the list of approved disinfectants) may be obtained from HM Stationery Office. Copies of the Northern Ireland Welfare of Animals Act 1982 and the Animal Boarding Establishments Regulations (NI) 1974 may be obtained from HMSO, 80 Chichester Street, Belfast BT1 4JY. Residents of Northern Ireland wishing to enquire about boarding establishments should contact the Department of Agriculture, Dundonald House, Upper Newtownards Road, Belfast, tel: 01232 650111.

LICENSING AUTHORITIES

There are a few boarding establishments situated on some of the smaller British isles and occasionally one of these may be offered for sale. The Isle of Wight is part of the county of Hampshire but has two district councils with authority to issue boarding kennel licences and inspect boarding establishment premises: Medina and South Wight District Councils.

In the Channel Islands, both Jersey and Guernsey have their own separate governments, and Guernsey's regulations usually extend to the island of Alderney. Neither Jersey nor Guernsey has any government regulations concerning small animal boarding establishments, though there are cruelty to animals acts in force under which their animal protection societies could act if requested. These are the Jersey Society for the Prevention of Cruelty to Animals and the Guernsey SPCA, whose work is similar to that of the RSPCA.

The Isle of Man has its own government and enquiries concerning boarding kennels may be made to the Animal Health Department, IOM Board of Agriculture and Fisheries, Douglas. The Animal Boarding Establishments (Isle of Man) Act 1973 is the relevant Act in force, and animal boarding establishments must be licensed and may be inspected by an officer authorised by the Board of Agriculture and Fisheries.

It is noteworthy that regardless of area and despite government Acts and inspection by officers of the district authorities, there is great variation in small animal boarding establishments, accommodation and administration. They vary from admirable to unacceptable – the abysmally awful now being very rare. For this reason prospective boarding kennel owners are advised to see as many kennel properties as possible even though they may be viewing establishments outside their chosen price range. Extensive viewing is necessary to see both the best and the worst – how else will you be able to set your own standard of achievement?

LIABILITY FOR DAMAGE

Others Acts of Parliament will apply to boarding kennel owners, depending on circumstances and conditions: for example, the Animals Act 1971, which applies in England and Wales only, makes provision for civil liability for damage done by animals, protection of livestock from dogs, and for purposes connected with these matters.

RETAIL TRADING

Should a boarding kennel owner decide to expand his or her business by selling dog and cat foods and pet accessories (for which planning permission may be necessary from the local authority if sales become more than an ancillary part of the business) the owner will be subject to the Weights and Measures Act and the Trade Descriptions Acts, and in addition will need to be familiar with the Feeding Stuffs Regulations 1982, which were implemented in July 1984.

The Feeding Stuffs Regulations 1982 are intended to protect the health of pets (*all* pets, not only dogs and cats) and to make it quite clear to pet owners what nature of food they are buying. Regulations concerning other animal foods, for pigs and cows for example, have existed for some time. These regulations affect the boarding kennel owner in two ways – in the food that they buy for their boarders and the food that they sell to their clients if the kennel also has a retail shop. Dog and cat food must display on its packaging the name and description of the food, state what animals it is intended for, give directions for use, state the net weight, show a list of ingredients in descending order by weight, and list certain additives. It is the responsibility of the company or person whose name appears on the pack to ensure that the information is correct; these regulations apply to compound foodstuffs, not 'plain' products such as fish or meat which are not part of a mixed food.

In a kennel shop, and in some pet shops, difficulties arise when some products – for example the particular dry dog food you serve to your boarders and want to offer to your clients when the boarder goes home – are sold loose because you have purchased it in 15 kg sacks but customers wish to buy it by the kilo. If a product is sold loose from a bin, bag or box, the relevant details concerning the food have to be displayed. If you prepack products into handy-size bags to display on shelves, the law states that it is not necessary to label every bag as long as the details of the product contents are displayed at the point of sale. It would be far better to make sure that pet foods sold loose are then packed in a container which bears a label stating the contents and how to use them. Most pet owners do not sufficiently understand the differences between complete and complementary foods, or that the amounts required by animals of some foods will not be the same as with other products. Solve this problem by dealing with manufacturers who market their products in small packs for pet owners as well as in large sacks for you!

Further details and current regulations are available from the Pet Food Manufacturers' Association (PFMA) www.pfma.org.uk, tel: 020 7379 9009.

TERMS FOR BOARDING

The most frequent point of civil law in connection with the boarding kennel business arises from dogs and cats being booked into a boarding establishment and not being collected at the end of their vacation. Most boarding kennel owners state on their booking form that if animals are not collected within 15 days of their due departure date, and no communication from the owner or the owner's agent is received, and if attempts by the kennel to contact them fail (kennels should have an emergency contact number for all their clients), the kennel reserves the right to dispose of the animals. Though the booking form, which should be signed by the pet owner and the kennel owner, is a contract, it is impossible to state definitely whether the 'right to dispose' clause may be implemented. This is a situation which is most worrying and happens far too frequently. It seems that some irresponsible pet owners choose this method as a soft option to abandon animals they no longer wish to keep. Sometimes boarding kennel owners find they have two or three pets for which no fees have been paid and which are occupying accommodation booked by another client.

Kennel owners should serve notices on pet owners to the effect that they owe a specified amount for the animal's board and that unless the account is settled within a specified time further action will be taken to collect the money and dispose of the pet(s). The kennel owner can apply to the magistrates' court for advice but it will cost money and still probably not recover the fees. It also costs to have animals destroyed by the veterinary surgeon, and there is the natural reluctance to take such a step anyway. Efforts can certainly be made to re-home them, though if they are sold it will most likely be at a considerable loss. It seems that kennel owners would be well advised to consult their own solicitors because of the complexities of contractual law. Another useful website is the court service moneyclaim at www.moneyclaim.gov.uk, which is an online service for those owed small amounts of money. In my own view, if every effort has been made to contact the owners, the animals have, in effect, been abandoned and are therefore the responsibility of the local authority. Discussion with your Environmental Health Officer or Dog Warden could be helpful.

It is too easy to say that such situations should be avoided. When a boarding kennel is well established it might be possible to ask that new clients settle their pets' boarding fees in advance, whereas known clients would not be asked to do so. However, new kennel owners will take a year at least to meet their 'regulars', though some information may be gleaned from their predecessor's records. In the course of what is admittedly inconclusive research (because the sample is necessarily a small one) it has been observed that in almost all cases of the abandonment of pets in boarding kennels the pet owners had housing difficulties. There are, of course, many genuine cases of house moving when it is desirable for pets to be boarded during the actual moving operation, and it can be very hard to differentiate between the genuine and the shady story. Similarly, pets often need to be boarded during the owner's hospitalisation, and in such circumstances some owners may be eligible to receive help towards boarding fees from the Social Services. Perhaps after a time every boarding kennel owner develops a sixth sense for these types of people, but almost every kennel gets caught at some time or other.

Certain types of kennels are exempt from inspection under the 1963 Animal Boarding Establishments Act. Some of these apparently exempt kennels may, in some ways, threaten a boarding kennel owner's business, but more direct threats appear from unlicensed quarters. The services offered by individuals who advertise pet walking/visiting services in the

BEERODE BOARDING KENNELS

Proprietors: J & M Doe

BEERODE
Nr ANYTOWN
Tel: Beerode 4321
Website: www.beerodekennels.com

BOOKING APPLICATION FORM

I accept Beerode Boarding Kennels' conditions of boarding as shown in their brochure and wish to board my dog(s)/cat(s)

From: ....To: ....
Owner's name: ....Tel: ....
Address: ....
Temporary address: ....
Address of contact: ....
Dog(s) names: ....Ages(s): ....
Breed or Description: ....
Cats(s) names: ....Ages(s): ....
Breed or Description: ....
Usual foods: ....
Usual veterinary surgeon: ....

NO DOGS/CATS WILL BE ACCEPTED WITHOUT A CURRENT
VACCINATION CERTIFICATE

I understand that while every care will be given to my animals, they are boarded entirely at my own risk. I authorise you to call a veterinary surgeon on my behalf should it be necessary. I enclose a deposit of £............. which I understand is not returnable if the booking is cancelled and that the boarding fees are due for the full booking should I collect my animals before the due date of departure.

Beerode Boarding Kennels reserve the right to dispose of animals not collected within 15 days of the stated departure date if no communication from the owner, or the owner's agent, is received, and if efforts to contact the owners fail.

Signed: ....Signed: ....
(Beerode Kennels)   (Owner)

pet owner's absence are outside the jurisdiction of the 1963 Act and consist of visits to the house to feed and exercise the pets which, apart from the visits, are left to their own devices. Organisations providing personnel to live in the home with the animal during an owner's absence are also outside the jurisdiction of the 1963 Act. Home boarding, however, is not. These services are discussed in more detail in Chapter 13.

6 Health Matters

Kennel owners need to be experts in cleaning and hygiene, and in training their staff to carry out these duties daily. Anything less than perfection in these tasks creates a foothold for the development of health problems. Kennel cleaning, unless properly understood and carried out, may have hazards of its own. The proper cleaning of kennels inevitably requires the use of chemicals, most of which will come under COSHH (Control of Substances Hazardous to Health) regulations and care must be exercised in their storage and use.

Always read the labels, and store and use cleaning chemicals strictly according to directions. Clear and precise instructions, particularly in respect of dilutions of chemicals, are essential, and clearly marked – separate – measuring jugs must be available for all liquids that need to be diluted. It is strongly advised that you purchase your kennel cleaning requirements from a company which specialises in chemicals formulated for use in the boarding kennel and the veterinary profession, as such companies are always available for advice if required. Your own veterinary surgeon should be able to recommend a suitable company. Keep a check on cleaning materials and re-order before stocks become too low. Do not hesitate to enquire from the manufacturers whether cleaning chemicals have any carcinogenic qualities, and if they do, choose another product if appropriate.

It should not be assumed that kennel assistants automatically know of the benefits, and hazards, of the cleaning and disinfecting agents they will be required to use, so they must be properly trained in their use and should, of course, be provided with protective clothing. Overalls, rubber gloves and wellington boots are basic essentials and protective eye glasses (plastic ones which can actually be worn over normal spectacles if necessary) are also a necessity. Just one small splash in the eye of any irritant from dish washing detergent to kennel disinfectant can be both extremely painful and dangerous. Should that type of accident occur, seek medical advice immediately. Kennel assistants must take cleaning chores seriously for the sake of their own health and safety as well as that of the boarded animals.

KENNEL CLEANING

Cleaning is a daily routine, a procedure which must be thorough despite any temptation to skimp on the job. This has to be impressed very firmly on new staff. The microscopic organisms which have caused serious setbacks to many kennels, and been the downfall of some, are always present. Micro-organisms can thrive and multiply in such places as around chips in enamel feeding bowls or on the frayed edges of chewed and battered plastic dishes, quite apart from the obvious corners. Proper daily cleaning plus regular super cleaning of kennels between one boarder leaving and the next taking up residence; the period 'spring clean', usually undertaken in the slack season or perhaps when one kennel block is not in use – all will help to keep micro-organisms (bacteria and viruses) at bay.

One element of disinfection is often overlooked. Dirt and debris negate the effect of most disinfectants. Surfaces, utensils and implements must first be thoroughly cleaned, then disinfected according to the manufacturer's recommendations and then left for *at least* 20 minutes before washing down. Swilling disinfectant about, unless the whole procedure is followed, is worse than useless because it gives a false sense of protection.

Tools and equipment

For the cleaning operations, brooms, brushes, dustpans and 'pooper-scoopers' are indispensable, and a vacuum cleaner with a long extension hose will remove dust which accumulates on high ledges. Buckets and mops, and stiff 'yard' brooms are other essentials and all these items should be heavy duty as they will take a lot of wear and tear. Each kennel block should have its own set of cleaning tools; in the case of disease breaking out in one block, the less interchange of equipment between blocks the better. Specialist equipment such as pooper-scoopers can be purchased from kennel suppliers whose advertisements will be found in the weekly dog papers, or may be available at dog shows or from some pet accessory suppliers. Kennel vacuum cleaners are probably those which have been displaced by fancier models in the house or purchased second-hand, the cylinder or industrial type being the most useful. Mops, deck scrubbing brushes, brooms and buckets should all be chosen for ease of use as well as durability, or there will be complaints such as housemaid's knee and aching backs to add to the problems of kennel ownership. Never overlook the usefulness of the watering can, either.

Garden hoses and convenient taps from which to run them, yes; but unless you have already been involved in kennel work you might not think of items such as pressure washers. These are industrial cleaning machines which can be used at low or high pressures, with hot or cold water or saturated steam. They may be used with a detergent, and can clean roofs and walls as well as floors. Naturally, inexperienced staff should not be expected to handle sophisticated equipment without training: steam cleaning may remove the paint and plaster as well as the dirt and germs!

There have recently been significant changes in regulations concerning the provision of water to commercial premises. There has always been the requirement that commercial water taps to which hoses may be attached should have a double non-return valve in the system behind the tap. The reason for this is that if there is an interruption to the flow of water from the mains, a vacuum can be created in the system, so that, if the tap is turned on and the end of a hosepipe is in surface or foul water, this can be sucked back up into the mains system. This is an unlikely scenario but it has happened, and European legislation now demands an air break between the mains supply and the hosepipe. This works like a toilet cistern (which is in place partly for the same reason), but the disadvantage to the kennel is that such a break means that the water pressure drops sharply and the flow is often not enough to carry out cleaning procedures properly.

There are a number of ways around the problem. The most effective (and the most expensive) is the water tower – a huge cistern that contains enough water and is high enough to ensure a sufficient flow and pressure. Lots of taps are another answer: so long as the hose is not long enough to reach the ground, there is no requirement to have the air break. Another solution is a pump-powered cistern, although the supply is limited and you would need one for each kennel block because they are too heavy to move about. A large water pressure washer, so long as the double return value is fitted to the mains source, may be suitable, but not all water authorities are prepared to accept them. Personally, I believe that this demand by the regulations is 'over the top', but the law is the law and we have to make provision for this demand.

Another cleaning item, essential in the kennel context, is the automatic washing machine. At one time, small kennels might have relied on the owner's washing machine to cope with the kennel laundry, but this is no longer acceptable. The second-hand sales rooms may have some useful bargains in this type of equipment and it can be quite inexpensive. There will be a constant stream of bedding and towels to wash.

Disinfection

Disinfection should not be confused with sterilisation, which means the destruction of all living matter, or with disinfestation, which is the destruction of vermin and pests. However, as previously explained, before disinfectants are brought into action on the kennel front, basic but thorough cleaning must be carried out. Dust, dirt, urine, faeces, coat and skin detritus are contaminants which may render some disinfectants inactive, as does the presence of detergent in certain cases. Antiseptics are products for use on the skin or living tissue and are not to be confused with products designed for cleaning floors, walls or utensils.

However major or minor the basic cleaning chores, surfaces should be rinsed clean of detergent and dried before the disinfecting process can be carried out efficiently. Too many kennel workers forget, or have never been taught, that cleaning comes before disinfecting, as dust and organic matter may render the disinfectant properties inactive.

Quarantine kennels, except in unusual cases, are not for beginners but may be in their plans for the future; they are required to use a disinfectant approved for use under the Diseases of Animals (Approved Disinfectants) Order 1978 (amended 1991 and 2004).

As suggested in Chapter 5, every boarding kennel owner should have a copy of the list of disinfectants approved by the Department for Environment, Food and Rural Affairs (Defra), because the products listed therein have been officially tested. Several are available through distributors of products for use in kennels, whose advertisements will be found in the canine and feline press. Also, the approved list gives the name of each disinfectant and the name and address of the proprietor. It is therefore a simple matter to contact them for information and advice on the use of particular products. Full details are available at www.defra.gov.uk/ animalh/diseases/control/disinfectants_enscot.pdf.

Products intended for agricultural use are not necessarily correct for use in small animal boarding establishments, but in some cases the same manufacturers also produce disinfectants specifically designed for use with dogs and cats. They have specific information regarding their use in domestic boarding kennels and catteries, and will advise you as to the chemical content of the disinfectant and of its correct dilution for its use in particular circumstances. Remember that the most expensive is not necessarily the best. Bleach remains the most effective all-round disinfectant and is very cheap but needs to be handled very carefully, and kennels must be thoroughly washed down afterwards.

In all cases it should be remembered that disinfectants are dangerous substances and that kennel staff must be properly instructed in their use. Disinfectants require time to work, and such times should be given in the instructions for use and carefully followed. Fumes from disinfectants are hazardous too and may cause respiratory problems in humans or animals. Liquids may soak into any permeable materials – that is, unsealed wood, brick or concrete – and heat, either natural or applied, may cause fumes to be released. This is one reason why impervious materials are advised in kennel construction.

The Feline Advisory Bureau also publishes a comprehensive list of disinfectants and advises on their use in catteries. Some disinfectants which are suitable for use in canine accommodation are not suitable for use with cats. The boarding kennel and cattery owner's objective is optimum health within the establishment, and some individual research into this subject should be rewarding.

Chemical disinfectants

Disinfectant agents are either physical or chemical. Steam is a physical agent and may be used in the kennel environment in pressure cleaners. A hot industrial pressure washer is an expensive item of equipment (£1,000–£2,000) but very effective. Most organisms are destroyed at temperatures over 70°C, so steam is a very effective disinfectant. Chemical agents are contained in disinfectants found on supermarket shelves or supplied by firms specialising in kennel disinfectants. The labelling of domestic disinfectants is not universally good despite improvements in recent years. It is now a requirement to show the chemical contents on labels of disinfectant containers, warnings regarding their misuse and what remedial actions should be taken in such circumstances, but no domestic disinfectants actually suggest kennel use, though some are suitable. Others may be safe with dogs but should not be used with cats. With one exception – bleach – it would be wiser to choose a disinfectant product specifically designed for use in kennels.

Each constituent of chemical disinfectants has its own characteristic; knowing how they should be used may help the boarding kennel owner to decide which products to choose. The efficiency of any disinfectant depends on several factors, including, of course, the micro-organisms which it will be required to eliminate, where the disinfectant is to be used and on what type of surface, whether it is toxic (poisonous) to some species, whether it may cause corrosion, or damage or irritation to the skin and tissue, and whether there is anything present in the environment (dirt, detergent, etc) which might inhibit its action. Two other factors need to be considered – expense and the competence of the person(s) who will be using the disinfectants. It should be stressed to kennel staff that disinfectants are to be used strictly in accordance with instructions, that dilutions must be correct, that one disinfectant should never be mixed with another, and that dish-washing detergent should never be added to a disinfectant solution in the false hope that it will aid cleaning power. It will, in most cases, simply render the disinfectant properties inactive! Disinfectants generally work better in higher temperatures; therefore they should be added to hot water.

Disinfectant chemicals are classified into simple generic groups: alkalis, alcohols, aldehydes, halogens, phenolics and surface-active agents. The groups from which the common disinfectants draw their constituents are the aldehydes (as formaldehyde solution – formalin), the halogens (sodium hypochlorite solution – bleach), and phenolics (phenol and its modern derivatives as found in such products as Jeyes Fluid, Jeypine, Lysol, Dettol, etc). The surface-active agents may be subdivided into two groups: quarternary ammonium compounds (Quats) and amphoteric/polymer surface-active agents. The latter sub-group contains the most modern of the disinfectant preparations, which, being both disinfectant and detergent, excel at cleaning while simultaneously annihilating the micro-organisms. Being non-toxic, non-corrosive, odourless, deodorising, harmless to the skin and not inactivated by organic matter, amphoteric/polymer surface-active agents meet many of the needs of the boarding kennel/cattery owner, and indeed are recommended for use in cat units. An example of the preparations available in this group is Tego, which is recommended by the Feline Advisory Bureau.

The more sophisticated disinfectants are combinations of various ingredients and are more expensive, but a properly protected kennel saves money in the end. As micro-organisms tend to develop resistance to chemicals, disinfectant formulae are always being researched and updated and new products introduced.

Bleach

Sodium hypochlorite (bleach) is very effective and is in regular use as a disinfectant in the domestic environment. Domestos is a well-known example and the manufacturers, Unilever, may be contacted at info@domestos.co.uk or by telephoning 0800 776645. The Domestos information pack includes a leaflet on pet hygiene listing the following dilutions which may be of use in boarding establishments: 4 fluid ounces Domestos per gallon of water for soiling on outside paths, tiled or vinyl-covered floors and litter trays. Feeding bowls should be washed in hot, soapy water and then disinfected by soaking in a solution of 1 fluid ounce Domestos per gallon of water for about 10 minutes, then rinsed thoroughly and dried. The second dilution may also be used for disinfecting pet beds, bedding, grooming implements, and toys and bedding where appropriate. (*NB:* 1 fluid ounce = 25 ml, 1 gallon = 4.5 litres.)

Please note that the above-mentioned dilutions refer only to Domestos, as not all bleaches have the same available sodium hypochlorite content. Another advantage is that to safeguard the environment Domestos breaks down rapidly after use into common salt, oxygen and other harmless substances. This underlines another point, namely that bleach should be mixed and used immediately, not left standing around for future use as it will become ineffective through oxidation, not to mention being a hazard to pets looking for a drink! Bleach must never be mixed with any other cleaner or dishwashing detergent and is inactivated by contact with organic matter, so if used in kennels and runs or litter trays, for example, these must be thoroughly cleaned of faeces, urine or other organic detritus before the bleach solution is used.

An ineffective use of bleach occurs when conscientious kennel owners, anxious to prevent visitors bringing infection into the kennels on their shoes, leave a doormat soaked in bleach at the kennel entrance. One pair of dirty shoes or boots on the bleach-soaked doormat inactivates the disinfectant properties, if indeed they have not already been inactivated by oxidation!

Bleach is readily available and comparatively inexpensive. It has many useful properties and some disadvantages, one being that it is not recommended for use on metal surfaces. However, there are advantages and disadvantages to all products, which demonstrates why, to assist you in making an informed choice, it is necessary to know the constituents of disinfectants and how they work.

Phenol

The other generic group from which the constituents of many well-known and easily obtained disinfectants are drawn is the phenolic group. Phenol, popularly called carbolic acid, is a caustic poison and extremely toxic to living tissue. Some of the modern derivatives of phenol are xylenol, chloroxyphenol, orthophenylphenol and hexachlorophene; residues of these substances can be absorbed through the skin and some of them have been banned from use in products designed for human babies. They are all dangerous to cats and should never be used in catteries. Many disinfectants in this group are used in boarding kennels for dogs and there have been many cases of sore paws and other problems which could be attributed to the use, overuse or incorrect use of unsuitable disinfectants. If there is any doubt that a product contains phenol, remember that water turns milky white when phenol is added to it.

Points to watch

There is a wide range of 'specialist' products on the market supported by impressive leaflets and public relations activity. 'New' is not necessarily better, so – read the label. Labels on all disinfectant preparations must list their chemical ingredients. Some products carry labels stating they are 'safe in use', or 'safe when used as directed', or 'safe for general household use'. None found on general sale is labelled as being 'guaranteed harmless to pets'. Even if such claims were made, some pets may be allergic to certain substances, and what may be suitable for dogs may mean death to cats. No boarding kennel owner, or anyone caring for animals, should purchase domestic disinfectants from any source without checking that the active ingredients are stated on the container. Proof of content, and official proof of testing in the small animal environment – not hearsay or salesmen's patter – are required because kennel owners' responsibility is towards the boarders in their care and to the owners of those animals.

Disinfectants with strong pine odours will soak into wood surfaces which have not been sealed, and should infra-red heat be used in the area, it will draw irritant fumes from the wood which may affect the pets' eyes.

It is most important to realise that dogs and cats in boarding kennels are of necessity confined to comparatively small spaces, and that apart from walking on surfaces which have been disinfected with possibly irritant chemicals, they may also lie on these surfaces; they may also lick themselves and thus ingest any disinfectant residue which adheres to their coats. Disinfected floors should always be rinsed with clean water and allowed to dry before the animal is put back into its kennel, and in our damp climate floor drying can be a problem. Direct heating to aid drying may cause fumes from an unsuitable disinfectant product. Squeegies are useful here. Described as 'broom handles with windscreen wipers instead of brushes', they can remove liquids from smooth surfaces very efficiently. The incorrect use of certain disinfectants which are generally unsuitable for kennels may also make kennel floors sticky; this is mainly due to the breakdown of the chemical constituents and their subsequent lack of efficacy.

Another problem is that if kennel staff do not understand the correct use of disinfectants, and why the manufacturers' recommended dilutions should be strictly adhered to, they may add disinfectants to a bucket of water making a stronger solution, which is not only unnecessary and wasteful but also a potential danger to a susceptible animal. A disinfectant noted for its efficacy in one field should not be automatically considered ideal for use in another. The general lack of comprehensive information on disinfectants and our common acceptance of these products without question is still a problem despite improved labelling requirements.

When boarding dogs and cats, use only disinfectant products proved suitable in the small animal boarding environment. Check that the dilution rate for use in a small animal environment is clearly indicated, that the active ingredient(s) are named and that a remedial procedure in case of accidents is shown. Instruct all kennel staff in the careful use of disinfectants, as the object must be to reduce the risk of disease without introducing health risks from the disinfectant agent.

Newcomers to the kennel business may not be familiar with the use of disinfectants in spray form. The specialists in kennel and cattery disinfectants can provide information on this type of product which, when sprayed into the air, helps to reduce airborne infection. Do not confuse these sprays with aerosols, which contain propellants, and which some animals absolutely loathe. An advantage of the spray disinfectants is the ease of use: spraying walls, floors, etc is time- and work-saving. Kennel work is physically hard, and effective labour-saving methods in any department are worth consideration. A great disadvantage of any spray disinfectant is that some pets and people who breathe in sprayed droplets may suffer from respiratory problems. Pets should not be present when spraying takes place, and kennel staff should wear masks.

Destroying worm eggs

There is one further useful, and some would say essential, item which a boarding kennel owner anxious to keep his or her establishment thoroughly disinfected should possess. This is the flame gun used for destroying weeds in the garden, which employs heat to destroy worm eggs. Much publicity has been given to the subject of *Toxocara canis* infection in children, and this is dealt with in more detail in Chapter 6. It might be hoped that all conscientious pet owners worm their dogs regularly, but even though more efficient worm medicines for pets continue to become available too many pet owners still do not take advantage of them.

The dogs in the boarding kennel may be shedding worm eggs, unknown to the kennel owners; the eggs are extremely tenacious, and can live even in raw concrete which is porous! Using a concrete sealant simply means that instead of invading the concrete, the worm eggs will be flushed off the sealed surface by the cleaning water or disinfectant and take up residence elsewhere. Disinfectants, unfortunately, do not kill sticky worm eggs, which can, however, be annihilated with a flame gun. Unsealed concrete runs can be treated annually with a flame gun after the main boarding season and when no dogs are around; this will remove the worm egg danger completely. When concrete runs or other stone surfaces have been sealed, it is necessary to check where the water runs off. Does it go straight down a drain? Does it run into a gravel soakaway which can be flame-gunned? Never embark on this annual operation unless all conditions are right and the hose is connected and ready, in case of fire.

INSECTICIDES

Insecticidal products are frequently used in conjunction with cleaning and disinfection, though not necessarily so. How much your kennel property is affected by flies, wasps and other airborne insects may depend on your daily cleaning routine, or by proximity to a farm, or neighbour whose attention to cleanliness is not as good as yours, or to other factors altogether. Again, it should be borne in mind that boarders are in a confined space, so spray the animal accommodation while the pets are outside! Insecticidal sprays need to be used with caution and the best choices are from the products made by the specialist kennel disinfection firms. Be sure that you and your staff know the difference between the various kennel air sprays, and when and how to use them. Never use any spray when there is food around, and always resist picking up the handy aerosol for a quick burst against flying intruders without considering what else is going on in the kennel. Many people, suspicious of the presence of too many chemicals sprayed into the atmosphere, prefer to use the old-fashioned sticky fly papers. These simple, unsightly but harmless objects are not easy to find these days, though they are usually advertised in the summer months in the weekly dog papers: kennel folk must be good customers.

EXTERIOR CLEANING

Having dealt with the interior cleaning of kennels, the same routine procedures can be applied to the runs attached to them. Ideally, each kennel should have its own adjoining run with free access. Even so, that is not sufficient for thorough exercise and the dogs look forward to a gallop in the larger paddock, where they are taken individually. Unfortunately, the Model Licence Conditions insist on a 'Kennel and Run' regime in newly built kennels, but many premises still retain the 'Pen and Exercise Area' regime that, despite the extra work involved both on moving dogs and keeping the areas clean, has many advantages, as explained in Chapter 5.

The large runs may be grassed, and if they are big enough they do not get too badly churned up in wet weather. Many dogs will not urinate or defecate except on grass; the disadvantage is the cleaning up! Some large exercise areas are surfaced with gravel or, better still, with washed pea beach. To surface large areas with concrete is costly and although they are the easiest to clean satisfactorily, dogs are usually much happier playing on grass, with gravel – once they learn to trust its surface – coming second.

Though grass or gravel runs may please the dog best, there is no way at all that they can be perfectly disinfected, however diligent the owner and kennel staff. Obviously, faeces should be removed from outside runs as frequently as necessary, and provided these are solid the task is not too difficult. The problems arise if a dog is afflicted with diarrhoea, which may be caused simply by stress while settling into new surroundings or, more seriously, by an illness. As it is impossible to tell immediately whether illness is the cause of the looseness, it is better to restrict the dog to an isolation kennel and clean and disinfect as required. This further points up the argument for having kennels with runs attached. Grass runs can be sprinkled with disinfectant applied from a watering can but efficient disinfection is an impossibility. The same applies to gravel, but regular 'picking up', as the expression is, plus spraying with the hose, will keep problems to a minimum. The MLCs require that such exercise areas are concreted, so grass and gravel will gradually be replaced.

STERILISATION OF FEEDING AND DRINKING BOWLS

A further daily cleaning routine is the proper cleansing and sterilisation of feeding and drinking bowls. A sterilising detergent is most useful here and is a time saver; it ensures a quick and thorough job. Otherwise, bowls can be washed in ordinary detergent, rinsed in clean water, then rinsed in a sodium hypochlorite solution and rinsed again before feeding time. Ideally each dog should have its own food and water bowls as a further precaution against passing on infections; alternatively, disposable dishes are available and these are particularly useful for cats. Stainless steel bowls are by far the best. Anything else is a false economy, although a few heavy cast-iron bowls are useful for dogs who delight in tipping over light bowls full of water.

The automatic dishwasher especially for kennel use has probably not yet been invented, but a commercial or domestic dishwasher is by far the most hygienic way of washing dishes and it is possible to pick up second-hand ones cheaply.

DISPOSAL PROBLEMS

Environmental considerations regarding waste disposal have received a great deal of attention in recent years so kennels cannot afford to choose anything other than the best and 'greenest' options.

The kennel owner's first disposal problem is how to cope with the inevitable daily accumulation of excrement, which is an inescapable fact of kennel life. Other kennel routines have some bearing on this problem, as does the question of whether or not your kennel is on main drainage or has its own cesspool or septic tank drainage. Kennel waste disposal is without doubt a major subject which new kennel owners need to study.

The first consideration should be how certain kennel routines may assist, or complicate, disposal problems. The choice of bedding material has a bearing on this subject, as has the use of newspapers or other coverings on kennel floors. The boarders which are pet dogs, one might fairly presume to have been house-trained; those which are strictly kennel dogs, from breeding kennels for example, may not be house-trained, though they should certainly be kennel clean; much depends on how their owners have educated them. There may be times when your boarding kennel cares for show dogs or breeding stock, as breeders/exhibitors need holiday breaks too and assistance in times of illness. The kennel owner who is connected with the dog show world may know what to expect behaviourwise from kennel dogs as opposed to household pets; the newcomer without this experience will have to learn the hard way.

The best-trained household pet, when subjected to stress, such as being marched off to the kennel, may suffer tummy upsets, and then suffer further stress because it has made a mess in its kennel. Rebukes for such mistakes are not to be administered in the boarding environment, where understanding of the reasons and a building of confidence as the boarder settles down improve the situation. Kennel owners and workers have to accept the fact that these least pleasant chores are most important. Working with animals involves all their care in sickness and in health; looking after the animals' living quarters, and the unrewarding, unpleasant and, at times, foul jobs are part of total care.

Beds and bedding

Pets in the boarding environment need to be happy, and bringing their own bedding keeps them in touch with home comforts. Some kennels forbid this, as they say there is always a problem if a favourite blanket is lost or damaged, but my view is that it is worth it if the dog settles more quickly. Some owners may even bring their pet's bed too, but you should always have available bedding and beds of varying sizes. It is also helpful when owners bring their pet's towel, but the wise kennel owner keeps a stock of towels on hand anyway – a spell of wet weather means a lot of wet dogs. Short-haired breeds are quickly dried, but some of the long-haired varieties need careful drying and, in fact, the use of an electric dog dryer or drying cabinet simplifies this task and it is a worthwhile purchase. Floor-standing electric dog dryers are, of course, standard equipment in any grooming parlour.

Bedding needs to be kept clean, and is not shared with other boarders unless two dogs from the same family are kennelled together. Sending a boarder home with soiled bedding will not endear you to the owner, which is bad for business, so your washing machine will be kept busy. A tumble dryer is virtually a necessity. Blankets are useful, and polyester 'fur' bedding is particularly cosy and comfortable and is fully washable. Flame-retardent materials exist and are an added bonus, as fire risks must be kept to a minimum. Because of the risk of fire, certain types of bedding should not be used in small animal boarding establishments. These include wood, wool and straw, which may also harbour insects.

Boarding kennel owners, and the boarders' owners too, need to be warned that some dogs in kennels are particularly destructive and set to work on reducing their bedding to shreds and wreck their beds if possible. Pet owners seldom take such things into account when they complain about your boarding fees! Some modern kennel designs include fibreglass beds which fold up into the walls, giving more kennel space – but if your kennel is so equipped, bear in mind that a dog needs something to rest on during the day.

Fibreglass is a 'warm' material and is also used for conventional beds which then need little if any bedding. Oval plastic beds are available in all sizes, stack well when not in use and are easy to scrub, but can get chewed around the edges. Remember that frayed edges of plastic beds will harbour germs just as do chewed edges of plastic feeding dishes. What is not so obvious is that beds with frayed edges will collect hair, particularly from long-coated breeds. There is something to be said for encouraging clients to bring their pets' own beds!

Cat trays and cat litter

Dogs are unlikely to soil their bedding unless they are ill, and many well-house-trained dogs will often be clean overnight even in the strange environment of a kennel. Others, however, if they need to urinate or defecate, will do so and get back into their bed and wait for the kennel staff to clean up in the morning. Cats, on the other hand, are almost always meticulous in their toilet routine. Without a tray containing a material that will absorb liquid and dry faeces and which can be used to cover up the sight and smell of their excrement, they can become ill as a result of their refusal to exercise their normal bodily functions. It is essential that cats have a tray (easily cleaned plastic or disposable) with a good layer of cat litter placed well away from their sleeping area. Experience shows that if the bed can be well above the ground and the litter tray on the floor most cats are comfortable.

As with most supplies, cat litter comes in a range of prices and you tend to get what you pay for. The most common in kennels, and the least expensive, are clay chippings, but materials range from condensed wood chippings to fine, highly absorbent, scented granules that clump densely together around both liquids and solids and can be lifted out easily, leaving only clean litter behind.

It is recommended that all litter trays are emptied and cleaned regularly. For many cats this may only be once each day, but others will require attention more often. For most materials this is essential, although if using the fine granules mentioned above, a deep layer of litter may be used with a complete change each week. If two or more cats from the same family share accommodation, it might be necessary to have two litter trays.

Floor coverings

Strictly speaking, the impervious and properly cleaned and dry kennel floor should need no additional covering. Whatever you put down as a floor covering will rapidly become untidy, if not ripped to pieces. However, there are occasions when some sort of covering may be needed and most kennels keep a stock of newspapers for such purposes. These can be saved from your household, scrounged from neighbours and friends, brought in by clients or begged from your local newspaper distribution depot. Broadsheet newspapers are much more effective than the tabloids or 'compacts'. Newsprint is mildly biocidal, which is an advantage, but unfortunately printer's ink will discolour light-coloured coats and make white dogs positively grubby.

Other points against the use of newspaper are the fire risk and the disposal problem. However, it is particularly useful for puppies, whose idea of toilet training may revert to the newspaper stage, and in cases of illness. Your isolation unit should have a supply in readiness. Needless to say, used newspaper should be destroyed, preferably by incineration.

Resist the temptation to scatter sawdust or woodchips on kennel floors, even though you may have seen such things in kennels which you have visited. The fire hazard rules these materials out, and there is an added risk of sawdust getting into dogs' coats or eyes and setting up skin irritations. If sawdust is used at all, it should only be from softwoods which have not been treated with wood preservatives. Products used for treating timber can be toxic to animals, and this should also be borne in mind if wooden cattery buildings are used. If possible, avoid the use of bedding materials and floor coverings which are potentially dangerous, create a disposal problem and therefore cause you extra work.

Incineration

Open incineration used to be an acceptable method for disposal of kennel waste, but recently much more emphasis has been accorded to air pollution and this method may not now be approved in some areas. Closed oil-fired systems are available but are expensive to buy and to run. Therefore, whether you are starting your own boarding kennel or are purchasing an existing business, disposal of kennel waste is an extremely important matter for consideration. In the case of an existing business, check whether the disposal methods used by the seller are approved by the local environmental health department, and if not find out what system would meet official approval. If you are starting your own kennel, discuss the waste disposal system with your environmental health officer before becoming involved. If possible, check with other boarding kennels regarding the efficacy of approved disposal systems. Do not underestimate the waste disposal volume from a busy boarding kennel and/or cattery, and remember that kennel and cattery waste awaiting disposal must be contained so that it does not attract flies. Heavy-duty black plastic bags may serve as temporary containers, but keep them out of sight if possible. Regular disposal of kennel waste is vitally important.

Cesspool and septic tank

One other competent disposal method for kennel excrement is via the septic tank or cesspool if a foul sewer is not available in your area. It is essential that you do not use the main drainage system unless you have a proper macerator or holding tank and the permission of the service supplier. Main drainage services are for domestic liquid waste and surface water only.

A cesspool which serves either the house or the kennels will need to be emptied by the local council or a private sewage disposal contractor, for which a charge will be made. A septic tank is a tank in which the solid matter of continuously flowing sewage is disintegrated by bacteria. These tanks have an overflow of clear water, usually draining down to a stream or ditch. In theory a septic tank is not supposed to need emptying, but in fact most require periodic attention. If the property you have taken over has septic tank drainage for kennel use, check the capacity of the tank – or rather, ask the person who comes to empty it, unless the capacity is listed elsewhere. Modern detergents, disinfectants and other chemicals play a part in inhibiting the bacterial action, which should keep the septic tank trouble free. The new country dweller needs to study rural drainage. Knowing how to cope with previously unfamiliar systems will help to obviate problems. Check where the pipes run; note where the overflow and soakaway are located; such areas can become overgrown with grass or nettles. In fact, a particularly luscious grass or weed growth in an otherwise sparse area should alert the warning signals in your brain. Check that an overflow is not blocked: if it is, seek help without delay.

It stands to reason that if they are available and working properly, septic tanks are the most convenient and least unpleasant means of kennel excrement disposal. However, no drains can be used for the disposal of soiled newspaper, sawdust, wood chips or cat litter, which must be burned. Companies specialising in kennel design and equipment have up-to-date information on modern disposal systems.

Remember that 'balance' is crucial. The addition of just a few kennels can overwhelm a system that has been adequate for years.

Refuse collection or burial

Dustbins and garbage sacks are other items of necessity. Not everything can be burned or disposed of via the septic tank. If canned dog or cat food is used, and some surely will be, the empty tins are for the refuse collectors. These tins can amount to a sizeable problem; one way of reducing the tin mountain is by opening the tin at both ends and then crushing it flat, which saves a great deal of space. Naturally, any refuse which has to await council collection should be in containers with tight lids. The local population of wild creatures, including foxes and badgers, will otherwise raid the garbage.

One further method of disposal of kennel waste is by burial. This is the most laborious and time-consuming operation and is often dependent on the right digging conditions or how much ground there is available. It can be satisfactory but is better avoided unless some member of the kennel crew wants to spend all his days digging. Other methods of disposal exist, none acceptable, and in fact some kennel owners prefer to remain secretive about their methods, which may therefore be viewed with suspicion. Never continue a highly suspect method of disposal just because your predecessor got away with it. Remember this is a health subject.

Much useful information is available on the website of the Office of Public Sector Information (www.opsi.gov.uk/acts). Search for the Clean Neighbourhoods and Environmental Act 2005.

HUMAN CONSIDERATIONS

Though the boarders come first, the humans owning or employed at the kennel deserve consideration too. The work is physically hard, which many enjoy; it is also repetitive, which some may find boring at times. The fact that the physical chores of cleaning and caring involve bending, stretching, lifting, carrying and being on the go all day means that muscles may be over-used and complain. Learn to pace yourself and, though diligent and conscientious, do not become a workaholic. Everyone deserves a break and works better afterwards. The temptation, when working for oneself, is to drive on and on, perhaps not realising what is happening until that nasty feeling of exhaustion has to be heeded. Remembering the creative side to any job – that is, making the business work and prosper while seeing your boarders are well and happy – offsets some tensions which, unalleviated, cause tiredness. Job satisfaction is important, but so is recreation.

Clothing

Clothing should provide comfort and protection, and appearance needs to be thought of too. Clothes chosen for their usefulness need not look as if they are the dregs of a jumble sale. Jeans and track suits can be neat and tidy, as can shirts and sweaters. Wellington boots are a necessity, and comfortable rainwear gets a lot of use in our damp climate. Changes of clothing are necessary in really bad weather, and if you have live-in kennel staff, means of washing and drying clothing in a hurry is vitally important. T-shirts and tabard overalls can be very colourful and attractive. Simple styles in easy-care fabrics are essential.

Kennels conscious of marketing their business now often invest in T-shirts, polo shirts and/or sweatshirts with the kennel logo printed on them. It gives staff a sense of identity and promotes a professional image.

Pollutants

Although kennel owners and staff are not confined to the relatively small quarters assigned to the pets, they are exposed to cleaning and disinfecting materials, insect sprays and air fresheners every working day. The boarders stay for only a limited time; the staff carry on regardless. Some people, and some dogs, are allergic to these substances.

When cleaning kennels, or in fact in any cleaning demanding the use of disinfectants, protective clothing *must* be worn. Provide rubber gloves and rubber boots. Consider carefully your choice of chemical cleaners – again your most comprehensive advice will come from firms specialising in the manufacture of products for kennel use. Where possible choose sprays which are not aerosols; the use of aerosols should be limited if they cannot be avoided completely. If flea aerosols have to be used, try to do this in the open air and not in the confined space of a kennel, and warn kennel assistants to avoid breathing the spray. A pet owner spraying one dog occasionally is far less exposed to pollutant chemicals than the kennel worker involved with a number of dogs needing flea treatment. Insufficient publicity has been given so far to the health of workers in this industry.

SAFETY FIRST

Keeping up appearances is important, so painting and decorating will form a large part of the kennel maintenance work, though not in the busiest boarding weeks. Many of the modern redecorating products are hazardous from the point of view of fumes, and every effort should be made to obtain non-toxic products. No lead-based paints, please, and to save work remember that, as kennel painting is an oft-repeated task, a good covering of one coat of emulsion will do just as well as a fancier product needing two coats or more.

All decorating and maintenance supplies and tools need to be kept in a place of safety, as do all bulk supplies of disinfectants. These are simply sensible precautions so that you know where to find what you want when you need it – which will usually be immediately – and to prevent accidental misuse of any products which might be harmful to humans and dogs.

Most premises have a shed for the storage of equipment and materials that are only used occasionally. They are usually little short of a rubbish dump! Make sure that everything has a place and is in it. It saves a great deal of time in the long run.

Fire

Fire precautions should be observed at all times, and fire extinguishers sited according to the recommendations of your local fire prevention officer, whose advice can be obtained by a telephone call to the Fire Department.

Every kennel should bear a large NO SMOKING sign, and this should be rigidly enforced and observed by owners, staff and visitors. Not only is there a fire risk but cigarette smoke is yet one more air pollutant which should not be inflicted on pets or people. This is one hazard which you can eliminate totally from your kennel. The recently enacted ban on smoking in public places should be extended to your whole working and reception area.

Tetanus

All people connected with kennel work should make sure that their tetanus inoculations are in order. Consult your own doctor about this, and make sure that all your staff are protected too. Tetanus immunisation is necessary as cuts and scratches are sure to beset kennel workers from a variety of causes, and animal bites are not the least of these. Dogs and cats should be handled properly to prevent bites and scratches, and it must always be remembered that a frightened animal may react quickly and unpredictably in a way unlike its normal behaviour. Teeth and claws carry germs, and in the event of a kennel worker being bitten or scratched, prompt washing of even the smallest wound with soap or detergent is essential and may prevent infection setting in. Cat bites and scratches often cause more severe reactions than expected, so every precaution is an obvious necessity.

First aid boxes

Although the owner takes all precautions against major accidents, there are sure to be minor ones. As well as a boarders' first aid box (ask your vet to advise on the contents of this) there should be a staff first aid box. Equip the latter with some antiseptic solution, sterile dressings, an eye bath, band-aids, scissors and whatever you consider necessary for first aid treatment. Include a note showing the local doctor's telephone number, as it will save time looking it up in the directory if you have to make an appointment in a hurry. Most injuries are minor, but in the case of bites a doctor's advice should be sought.

Alternative medical care

Working in kennels is demanding and repetitive and may lead to strains and sprains or 'slipped discs'. To assist a fast return to work, effective treatment for such injuries may be given by a chiropractor or osteopath, and it is not usually necessary to be referred to a practitioner by your doctor. Consult the Yellow Pages. Fully qualified chiropractors have the letters DC after their names and are members of the British Chiropractic Association. Fully qualified osteopaths bear the letters DO MRO, which signify membership of the General Council and Register of Osteopaths. Newer members of these professions may also have a Bachelor of Science degree. Though not usually available under the NHS, such treatments are not excessively expensive and emergencies are usually seen without delay. Getting back to work quickly can save you money.

ZOONOSES AND OTHER AILMENTS

Zoonoses are diseases which are transmissible from animals to man. The most widely publicised of these is rabies and our quarantine kennels and our Pet Passport system are our front-line defences against this dreadful disease. Every kennel owner should obtain the Feline Advisory Bureau's excellent paper entitled Zoonoses, a copy of which should be in every kennel and cattery in the country. Do not be misled into thinking that this publication is only for cat enthusiasts. Some zoonoses have received an overdose of publicity considering their relatively low incidence. A few of them are mentioned here, but for detailed and up-to-date information please obtain the FAB paper.

Ringworm

Both dogs and cats may be infected with ringworm, a skin disease, and this is readily transmitted to man from the animals, but not from man to man. To be awkward, ringworm spores may not cause the dog or cat to show any symptoms, though infected animals can be diagnosed by the veterinary surgeon using an ultra-violet light known as a Wood's lamp. Any such infections, should they be attributed to your kennel, must be dealt with under veterinary direction, as it is a sure business loser apart from being an undesirable health risk and unpleasant for the sufferers.

Nematode worms

Everybody knows that dogs and cats have worms and that in comparatively rare cases – and they are very rare despite occasional alarmist publicity in the national press – a child may be affected by toxocariasis. The nematode worms *Toxocara canis* and *Toxocara cati* occur in dogs and cats and are passed in their faeces. Unfortunately, these eggs can survive in a viable state for several years. Adult animals may get worms by ingesting infective eggs, or by eating small mammals which are infected, and puppies and kittens become infected before they are born or as suckling babies. If man accidentally ingests the eggs, there may be infection of the central nervous system, or a sense organ such as the eye, resulting in partial or complete blindness. Some cases are reported annually in the UK and children are particularly vulnerable if they play in gardens or areas fouled by dogs. Uncontrolled dogs foul children's play areas in parks and this has resulted in the banning of dogs from some parks and beaches. It is unlikely that children would become infected at your kennels as they will not be playing in the dog runs, and your hygiene programme should minimise risks to visitors. Kennel owners are experts in cleaning up; most pet owners ignore the necessity!

Fleas

Dogs and cats have fleas. All dogs and cats may catch fleas from hedgehogs, or from each other, and fleas also bite people. It seems that human females are more likely to be the target of flea bites than human males. Some people react quite strongly to flea bites, others seem to be less bothered. Some dogs are extremely sensitive to flea allergens and suffer skin eruptions of the wet eczema type. Fleas are adaptable creatures and many a comfortable, centrally heated home has become a flea haven as fleas do not spend all their time aboard the animal but return for a quick meal as required. Wage war on fleas, as neither humans nor animals enjoy their company. Fleas live in carpets and in cracks between floorboards or in nooks and crannies in kennels.

Cheyletiella mange mite

Another minute pest has caused many people connected with small animal care a great deal of trouble because the real problem has often been difficult to diagnose. This is the cheyletiella mange mite, which may be suspected if a dog is very scurfy around the head and neck, is itchy and if, after cuddling such an animal, the human develops a rash similar to a crop of mosquito bites. Not everyone is allergic to the bites of the cheyletiella mite, though many owners who cuddle an infested puppy will be bitten on the arms and trunk, and on the thighs if they have let the puppy sit on their lap. These mites can be abolished by using a prescribed preparation such as Quellada veterinary shampoo. The cheyletiella mite also infects rabbits: hence its other name, the rabbit fur mite, and the difficulty of eliminating it.

Toxoplasmosis

Toxoplasmosis is another disease which has received wide publicity recently, and although infections with *Toxoplasma gondii*, a protozoan parasite, are common in man, the actual clinical disease is rare. Cats can play a key role in this disease as they may acquire infective cysts from meat and later shed infective oocysts in their faeces. The cat may show no symptoms whatsoever. Man may also acquire infection by eating cystic forms in meat, particularly if it is insufficiently cooked, and serological surveys indicate that 30 to 60 per cent of the adult human population have encountered the infection. However, it is important for pregnant women to avoid infection and they are made aware of this in literature pertaining to their condition. They should avoid handling cat litter.

Sarcoptic mange

Sarcoptic mange occurs in dogs and is transmissible to man in the form of scabies. This type of mange usually starts on the dog's muzzle and spreads backwards. When any skin conditions are noted in the dog or cat boarders, veterinary advice should be sought and the owner informed. It is surprising how many people think their pets are simply enjoying a good scratch without ever checking to see why they are scratching or uncomfortable.

Salmonella

The salmonella groups of bacteria are usually the culprits in most cases of food poisoning in man; such bacteria may be excreted by carrier animals who are quite well themselves, and most pets could be a possible source of infection. Fresh meat is also a possible source of salmonella and should always be handled with care, all cutting and preparation utensils being sterilised. There should never be direct contact between pet meat and meat intended for human consumption, or between cooked and raw meat.

It is, of course, important to be aware of the diseases which can be transmitted from animals to mankind but it is also important not to become obsessed by them. Proper, hygienic handling and attention to cleanliness can eliminate most dangers, and taking action against parasites can destroy that particular problem. The most difficult cases are those in which a person is allergic to cats or dogs in general and may suffer from asthma as a result. This cannot be called a true zoonosis, but it is a fact which cannot be ignored. Some people who are allergic to cats or dogs may have a reaction similar to hay fever, but, as with asthma allergy, tests by a doctor can determine the cause of the reactions. Unfortunately, such people often cannot work with cats and dogs.

Immunisation

There is one rule concerning your kennel which must never be broken – not even slightly bent; no boarders should ever be accepted without positive proof of vaccination. Not only should the boarders have been vaccinated against the prevalent infectious diseases but the immunisation record should show that it was carried out. For many years it has been taken as read that all dogs and cats should have booster vaccinations every 12 months, but recent research indicates that if a dog or cat has been fully vaccinated as a puppy or kitten, booster doses throughout its life may not be necessary, and indeed may be damaging to the health of the animal. Many veterinary surgeons are now taking this view. It is likely that the secondary legislation that will accompany the new Animal Welfare Bill will take this research into consideration when it is drafted. Again, the Model Licence Conditions insist that four weeks is the *minimum* time between the vaccination and it becoming effective, but this requirement is now considered unnecessary so long as the pet was fully vaccinated as a puppy or kitten. EHOs may still have the expectation of annual boosters and may still insist on annual boosters ('It's in the book!'). Otherwise, kennel owners may waive or qualify (to two, three or more years for boosters) the 12-month rule if the original vaccination certificate has been properly completed. When a dog or cat is vaccinated by a veterinary surgeon, a certificate of vaccination is given to the owner; this will indicate the date of the vaccination, the vaccine which was used and its batch number, and the diseases against which the pet was vaccinated. Accept no excuses for non-presentation of this document.

Dogs should have a certificate indicating that they have been immunised against canine parvovirus disease, distemper, hardpad and leptospirosis (CpDHL). Cats' certificates should indicate immunisation against feline enteritis and feline influenza. Subject to the above, should a vaccination certificate be within a short time of its renewal date when the pet's holiday booking is made, it would be sensible to advise the owner to consult the veterinary surgeon about the booster dose being given before the animal arrives at your kennel. A new location is always a challenge germ-wise, and boarding is also stressful for the pet, when it may be more vulnerable to disease than it would be in its own home surroundings.

In recent years parvovirus disease in dogs has been a major problem and when it first struck there was no specific vaccine for canines. However, great advances have now been made and boarding kennel owners should keep abreast of new developments in the prevention and treatment of infectious diseases. Regular news of this type is published in the weekly canine and feline press.

At the time of writing, the consensus is that puppies which have been inoculated against canine parvovirus disease at 8 and 12 weeks should be inoculated again at 18 or 20 weeks of age as it appears that some puppies carry a maternal immunity longer than others; if this inherent immunity is still present when a vaccination is given, it renders the vaccine ineffective. When in doubt seek a veterinary surgeon's advice. In the world of dogs it is generally the exhibition fraternity who are more aware of this, as their dogs are exposed to greater disease risks at shows. It is also possible that the pet dog which is taken for walks at the earliest possible opportunity may have acquired a certain 'street' immunity not shared by the more protected show pup. However, should you be asked to board a puppy, and dogs are puppies until they are a year old, check the date of its parvovirus vaccination and if there is any question in your mind about adequate protection, ask the vet about a booster injection.

There are many canine and feline illnesses of which boarding kennel owners should be aware, but it is not their job to diagnose or prescribe treatment for any ailments. This is the province of the veterinary surgeon and it is actually illegal for an unqualified person to infringe it. However, should the owner of a pet which boards with you provide medication prescribed by the dog's or cat's vet, it is your duty to make certain the vet's instructions are carried out. If a boarding kennel owner is not familiar with such conditions in dogs as pancreatitis, which involves a special diet, or diabetes, which may involve daily injections, it would be better to refuse such clients until sufficient knowledge and expertise in dealing with these cases have been acquired.

The most important observations a boarding kennel owner must be competent to make concerning a dog's or cat's health on arrival are whether there are obvious signs of illness. Does the animal look well? Does it have poorly eyes, a runny nose? Is it coughing? Limping? Has it any sores? Is it scratching itself? It is also important to realise that a dog which appears to be perfectly well on arrival may be incubating a disease which will manifest itself during the time it is boarding with you. The same warning applies to cats, but there is nothing you can do about this except to be aware that it might happen, and should it happen, take immediate action: isolate the pet and call the vet! Then follow his instructions to the letter.

For obvious reasons, it should be part of the routine when a pet comes into kennels that a 'health check' is completed. Ideally, this should be carried out in the presence of the owner, so that any problems with ears, eyes, matted coats, scurf or skin problems can be pointed out *before* the pet comes into the kennel and added to the animal's record.

Kennel cough

The bane of a kennel owner's life is kennel cough – a term which describes an upper respiratory infection only too commonly found in kennels. The chief symptom is, as the name suggests, a cough which may be aggravated by exercise or excitement, or possibly by apprehension. Sometimes it is a harsh dry cough, occasionally more like a choking cough, but, unfortunately, it is often a long-lasting cough, and the boarder which goes home coughing and spluttering will not endear your establishment to its owner. Discuss with your vet what you can do to minimise the risks of kennel cough, and remember that this disease is hardest on very young or elderly dogs. Kennel cough is highly infectious and veterinary advice should be sought immediately, both for the sake of treating the sufferers and to prevent the disease spreading if possible. Do not be tempted to ignore it, and discuss with your vet the possibility of vaccination against this disease.

The major cause of kennel cough, tracheobronchitis, is *Bordetella bronchiseptica* and dogs can be protected by an intranasal vaccine, Intrac, which protects for up to six months. Unfortunately, recovered dogs remain infectious for several months, so it is wise for all boarders to be protected. Some kennels insist that dogs coming onto the premises are protected against this particular form of the disease and report that the incidence has declined significantly and, in some cases, has been eliminated. Incidentally, the Intrac vaccination is considered effective in five days – not the four weeks required for full CpDHL vaccination.

Stress

Probably the most common cause of illness among the residents in a boarding kennel is stress. The pet is, without its consent, removed from its familiar surroundings and people, taken from its usual animal, human and geographical contacts and deposited in a different environment in close association with strange animals. Its mental and physical reactions are challenged. Stress reactions may vary in small animals as they do in the human animal: the animal is disturbed, it may be resentful, frightened and feel really ill. Hopefully it will settle down, perhaps with a little extra attention at first, and then thoroughly enjoy its holiday.

What sort of stress reactions might you expect from a dog or cat? Apart from an obvious wariness of the new surroundings there may be an initial refusal of food. If the refusal continues, then special care has to be initiated. Perhaps the dog or cat does not like the food offered, and it is for this reason that your booking form should include the question regarding the animal's usual diet. Sometimes an extra tasty titbit may induce the boarder to start its meal. Occasionally very special attention may be needed, in which case hand feeding is sometimes necessary, as it not only ensures that some food is taken but gives the stressed boarder that extra loving contact which it is obviously missing.

Stress can bring a bitch into season, though she may not be due; it can also have the opposite effect and a bitch arriving in season may promptly finish. Diarrhoea may be another stress symptom. No symptom should be lightly dismissed: if there is no rapid improvement, veterinary advice should be sought.

Ear problems

A dog's ears should not be itchy, sore, smelly or discharging. If they are, seek advice. Do not start pouring powders or squirting gooey liquids into a dog's ears unless you know why, otherwise you could make the problem worse. It is not your job to diagnose or prescribe treatment. Remember that.

Eczema

Dogs which come to board with you may not appear to be suffering from stress, or at least not as far as you can see. Unfortunately, they may suffer inwardly and sometimes skin eruptions occur. Also, the presence of fleas may cause some dogs to break out in 'wet eczema', a nasty, oozing, painful sore patch. Such dogs may be reacting to flea allergens. Seek veterinary advice right away. Certain antibiotics work particularly well on the skin and your vet will know what to prescribe.

Eye problems

Eyes should be bright and alert. If they are runny, dull or the 'haw' (third eyelid or nictitating membrane) is showing, be suspicious. This is particularly important in cats, but in any case be watchful and ask the vet's advice.

Medication and dangerous substances

Never give medicines to any dog or cat without specific instructions either from the owner who leaves a prescription with you or from your own veterinary surgeon. Medicines affect different dogs in different ways – a pill which may leave a small Poodle still active may send a large Afghan to sleep immediately. What suits one breed may be a disaster for the next. Medicine suitable for dogs may spell death for cats. Even simple diarrhoea mixtures which soothe one patient may merely mask the symptoms of a serious complaint in others, or could even kill a cat.

Though you may notice worms in a dog's or cat's faeces, you, as a boarding kennel owner, are not entitled to prescribe or administer medication without advice, and this is important, for worm medicines have been known to have adverse reactions. Do not take chances: take advice. Never look on a medicine as being harmless and beneficial to all species.

Apart from the irresponsible use of disinfectants, insect sprays, etc and the dangers of drugs and medicines mentioned above, other dangerous substances which your boarders could come into contact with are herbicides (if you have used weedkillers), paints (if you have used lead-based paints), and creosote (which might have been used to preserve wooden buildings or fence posts).

DANGEROUS DOGS

The Dangerous Dogs Act 1991, and amended in 1998, placed restrictions on the importation, breeding and owning of Pit Bull Terriers which are bred as fighting dogs, and the Japanese Tosa, of which only one example was imported into England. There are provisions in the Act to add other breeds should it be deemed necessary. The regulations and interpretations of the Act and its amendments are under continuous scrutiny and a number of changes in procedures have been put in place by some police forces.

Dogs that have been seized by the police under this legislation have to be kennelled somewhere and some experienced kennel owners have contracts with the local force to look after such dogs. Unfortunately the legislation emphasised what a dog looked like rather than its behaviour, and many of these dogs are not dangerous at all.

Whereas the Act itself may not affect the boarding kennel owner who is not personally involved with any breed initially restricted, much publicity has been given to terrible cases of people, and young children in particular, being savaged by large, powerful breeds such as the Rottweiler, the German Shepherd and other dogs of the guarding breeds. However, not all big dogs are dangerous. For example, the Guide Dogs for the Blind Association successfully uses large dogs, German Shepherds, Labradors, Golden Retrievers and crosses of the last two breeds when properly trained.

Unfortunately, human social problems have tempted some owners with little or no knowledge of training to acquire 'guard dogs', which are kept in a domestic environment unsuited to the dog's temperament. Any dog when challenged, startled, provoked or tempted is liable to bite, and aggressive large dogs with powerful jaws can inflict terrible damage. It is the few dogs which have reacted dangerously in certain circumstances, whether provoked or not, which inevitably have created a bad name for their breed in general. Small dogs are just as ready to use their sharp teeth in defence or aggression in certain circumstances.

How should the boarding kennel owner deal with dangerous dogs?

1. First, remember that not all members of so termed 'dangerous' breeds are aggressive, and second, never forget that any dog may bite.
2. Dogs tend to jump up when they bite; the larger the dog, the more powerful its jaws and the higher it can spring.
3. A lone dog in a single-person household may become very possessive of its owner and may resent attention from others such as kennel assistants.
4. Two or three dogs which live happily together at home, and therefore may be kennelled together, may fight in your boarding kennel. Anyone who interferes between fighting dogs is almost certain to be bitten!

5. Dogs, particularly males, may act aggressively towards a male dog in a neighbouring run, and therefore to anyone who interferes. Move one of these dogs to another kennel.
6. The management of dogs, dangerous or not, is simplified in kennels which have attached runs with access via a hatch which can be controlled from outside the kennel. Kennel doors which have provision for placing food and water bowls in position without the attendant having to enter the kennel itself are both time saving and a protection against aggression from the occupant. Some kennel gates are constructed on this principle.

Difficult pets

There are, unfortunately, some pets which are very difficult to handle. Though you may prefer to refuse to board certain breeds, some quite innocent-looking pets may display bizarre or dangerous behaviour unexpectedly. For example, the author was once severely bitten by a tiny toy dog and the owner's only comment was, 'He's such a brave wee doggie; he sometimes sits on the stairs and won't let us go up or down.' Bad behaviour in their pets is often tolerated, or even encouraged, by unwise owners.

Normal pets are sociable creatures and while an instinct to protect their property is understandable, unwarranted or unpredictable behaviour towards humans is unacceptable. Sometimes illness, a brain tumour for example, may cause behavioural changes in a dog. Some dogs may be disturbed by strange surroundings, your boarding kennel for example.

There are timid dogs and nervous dogs, and kennel staff should be trained to notice any change in a boarder's behaviour. Much more research has been done recently into the subject of animal behaviour and a book such as *Think Dog* by the late John Fisher and available from *Our Dogs*, gives valuable insight into dog behaviour and much advice regarding the handling of difficult dogs.

While most cats are placid pets, a few may be very nervous and require gentle care. There are also a few cats which can be very resentful or even downright spiteful in strange surroundings. Again, this bad behaviour may be tolerated by their owners. A pair of heavy gauntlets is a useful protection from sharp claws!

Recent research has indicated that there is a significant correlation between animal abuse and domestic violence. If a kennel owner suspects cruelty to a pet, then it is not just the RSPCA that should be informed: the NSPCC should also be notified.

The Animal Care College, among its range of courses, has programmes to help those involved in the industry understand the psychology of dogs and cats as well as modules on Health, Welfare, and Handling and Restraint.

7 Feeding the Boarders

The boarding kennel owner should understand the nutritional needs of dogs and cats; remember that when they arrive at the kennels they will be under stress and that animals, like people, react to it in different ways.

Kennel owners whose booking application forms require details of the pet's usual food report that the majority of dogs and cats are fed on canned or pouched food, plus, in the case of dogs, a biscuit mixer meal or whole-meal kibble – foods which are available at every local grocery store or supermarket, and not a bad feeding programme provided good-quality brands are chosen. This is still the norm, but there is no doubt that the 'complete' feeds are taking over rapidly as their convenience outweighs their price. Naturally there will be some owners who feed their dogs on the best steak, offer nothing but liver or fillet of sole, thinking, quite erroneously, that their pets are having the best. Others will use butchers' 'pet mince', a food of variable, and sometimes doubtful, value. Some pet owners, when preparing for their holiday, empty the family refrigerator of its collection of leftovers and feed them all to the dog in case it does not get a good meal in their absence! This means the pet may arrive on your doorstep full of unaccustomed goodies, and the initial shock of finding itself 'abandoned' by master or mistress may result in the pet starting its holiday with a very upset stomach. Owners may arrive with dog or cat and a carton of food, explaining that it is the only thing the pet will eat, or that it is the only food which does not give it diarrhoea. Surprisingly enough, the pet usually does very well on your kennel feed, but at least its home menu is there if required, and would of course be given if circumstances so dictated.

Another group of boarders falls into the special diet category. These may be dogs with a pancreatic disease or diabetes, or those on an obesity diet. Their diets will have been prescribed by veterinary surgeons and must be adhered to without deviation; these dogs may also require prescribed medication. You may impose special charges in such cases, or you may prefer not to cope with such problems. Sometimes it is preferable for a pet under treatment to be boarded with a veterinary surgeon as a hospital patient, but boarding kennel owners who have had experience in small animal care or animal nursing should be able to cope very well.

It sometimes happens that a client will claim that the pet will eat only an extravagant diet. In such situations, it is better to invite the pet owner to bring the food along; packed in daily portions and stored in a freezer it will present no bother to the kennel owner, though again, some may consider making an extra charge for 'special services'. It is also quite likely that, given the opportunity, the pet may thoroughly enjoy what all the other boarders are lapping up at mealtimes. Nevertheless, allowances must be made for pet food fads, and in some cases the customer really is right.

As the new owner you have an important choice to make when you take over a kennel. The easiest approach to feeding is to have a 'kennel feed' that you use for all the dogs and cats boarded with you. This often works well (with the provisos mentioned above) and there is a cost saving using a nutritious and economical food and buying it in bulk. However, as a service to clients and to their pets, more and more kennels are providing a range of popular foods and feeding whatever the pets normally eat at home. This is obviously a more expensive and time-consuming approach, but clients like to think that their pet is being looked after as closely as possible to its home conditions and offering such a feeding regime can give you an edge over other kennels in your area. The other advantage is that you are much less likely to experience feeding (and stomach) problems that sometimes occur with a change of diet. Just as important, the client will not experience any upsets when their pet returns home and resumes its normal, perhaps richer, diet. Owners who feed a less popular or, perhaps, a more exotic diet are asked to provide their pets' own food when they are booked in.

You also need to give attention to storage facilities. It is essential that your food stores (and refrigerators and freezers) are arranged in such a way that new stock coming in can be stacked in such a way that the most recently delivered food is used last. Routines must be in place to ensure that all new stock is placed, stored and stacked behind older stock. Even though tins, dry, moist and frozen foods have relatively long shelf lives, it is all too easy to leave a sack, tray or pack at the back of a storage facility. Apart from the fact that such stock handling procedures are good practice in themselves, you can be quite sure that your friendly Environment Services Officer will discover forgotten food during the annual inspection!

Your basic kennel feed needs to be palatable, nutritious, economical and easy to prepare and serve. Most adult dogs in normal health are used to being fed once a day, though there may be a few exceptions, with perhaps a biscuit or two either first thing in the morning or last thing at night, depending on the scheduled time of the main meal. Cats in normal health should be fed twice daily, but much more care is needed in planning their diets as they tend to suffer more from stress, particularly if they are boarded in a mixed kennel. Very young or elderly dog or cat boarders may need to be fed smaller quantities more frequently.

Some boarding kennels prefer to feed the dogs twice a day, early in the morning and in the late afternoon. They feel that this keeps the pets more contented and is also a precaution against bloat, or torsion, to which some breeds are particularly prone. Feeding only one main meal a day may lead to some dogs bolting their food, perhaps swallowing a lot of air in their hurry and thus causing discomfort or, at worst, bloat. Such a routine may mean that you should board fewer dogs, or employ more help. Either decision could necessitate a rise in your charges, but while there are pet owners who think all boarding fees are too high, there are many others who appreciate the extra care and attention given to their pets and are willing to pay for it. Needless to say, all dogs must be checked after each meal when you collect their empty dishes, and before bedtime, whatever feeding schedule you decide upon.

TYPES OF PET FOOD

Boarding kennel owners are now able to rely solely on manufactured pet foods should they wish to do so, and the cooking of pet foods and its attendant odours can be eliminated from the kennel chores. Not that all kennels will wish to cut out the cooking; it may depend on whether they have available suitable sources of fresh meat. The kennel owner should always be prepared to do some cooking for the boarders in case of necessity (usually boiling a chicken and rice for those recovering from digestive upsets). However, the time- and labour-saving method is to use a commercially prepared food, or foods from reputable manufacturers.

Several very well-known pet food manufacturers have spent millions of pounds in researching their products and testing them; from these people come not only excellent pet foods but also much of the research into animal nutrition, which means healthier lives for pets. In general it is best to deal with reputable, established manufacturers either directly or through their agents.

Dogs' diets do not need to be varied, as so many pet owners feel they should, and so the same food is acceptable day in, day out, and in fact a food regime which has been found suitable should be followed without alteration, because a sudden change of diet can lead to an upset stomach.

Therefore, you may be reassured, or even relieved, to know that once you have decided on a basic menu and routine of feeding you need not change it as long as it is satisfactory in the majority of cases. There may always be the occasional dog or cat which refuses outright to fit into your programme, or at first anyway. In such instances your duty is to the animal, not to your regime. For this reason, in addition to your normal foods you should be prepared with some extras tucked away in a freezer or stored suitably – for example, frozen chicken, chicken mince or rabbit, which must be cooked; tins of sardines or pilchards which are particularly tempting for some cats, and also for finicky dogs; perhaps small tins of rice pudding – the sort of things the pets might have at home. In cases of real difficulty, it might be worth remembering that some pets always finish the custard, and others are given the remains of the cereal and milk at breakfast time. Not part of the standard boarding kennel fare but very much part of home life, and if a boarder is very disturbed and disinclined to eat, provided there is no other apparent reason for lack of appetite, it is worth trying a few home treats in the hope that the pet will adjust to a more normal eating pattern. There is usually no need to panic if a new arrival refuses to eat on the first day.

How will you make your choice when deciding on a basic kennel food? It will be wise to consider the various types of dog and cat foods which are produced commercially in a ready-to-serve form, remembering that dogs tend to be omnivorous in their feeding habits but that cats are obligate carnivores. In short, cats *must* have meat in their diets because it is the only source of the essential amino acid they need. Dogs may prefer meat but can make good nutritional use of other forms of protein including vegetable protein.

Commercially prepared pet foods fall into three main categories.

CANNED FOOD

The one most generally known to pet owners is canned pet food, now often sold in the more convenient (and more expensive) foil pouches, which is preserved by heat sterilisation and therefore does not present the salmonella risks of fresh meat. It keeps in good condition for a long time. It contains a considerable proportion of water and although some canned food is labelled as being a complete diet, because cereal has been added, others may need to be mixed with soaked or dry biscuit meal to make a nutritionally complete meal for dogs. Canned meat for cats is nutritionally complete as it is and may be served without any additions. Most pets are used to a canned food diet; these foods are palatable and, if used correctly, easily digestible. The problems are the time it takes to open numbers of tins, and the disposal problem once they are empty, although we are now urged to recycle them.

SEMI-MOIST FOOD

The second type of commercially prepared pet food is known as 'semi-moist'. It is usually sold in packets, often containing inner packs of individual portions, and may have the appearance of mince or meat chunks. It is obviously not the real thing, but the dogs and cats do not seem to mind the rather plastic appearance of the food, which is prevented from spoiling by the addition of humectants and mould inhibitors. Semi-moist foods are readily available in the UK for dogs and cats, and such foods are complete and need no supplementation.

COMPLETE DRY FOOD

The third type of commercial pet food is known as 'complete dry food'. These foods are cereal based with the addition of meat and fish meal and contain almost no water. The cheapest ones may be presented in flake form as the processing is less complicated, but these are sometimes less easy to digest. Some complete food may come in a very hard pellet form which some dogs, particularly the smaller breeds, appear to find much too tough and obviously do not care for. Another presentation is an expanded, crunchy pellet form which most dogs enjoy. There are also complete dry foods for cats, but these have been, and to a certain extent still are, somewhat controversial. A pet which is fed on dry foods needs to drink a great deal more water than if it is fed on canned or semi-moist products; it is said by some that cats may not drink enough water when fed complete dry food and thus become susceptible to urological problems.

Complete foods for pets are nutritionally balanced and may form the sole diet of the dog or cat, with the proviso that boarding catteries must never use a complete dry food as the sole food for cats if the cats are not used to it. Such diets include vitamin and mineral supplements, so additions are unnecessary. Under the Feeding Stuffs Regulations Act 1982, the contents of pet foods, whether complete or complementary, must be listed in descending order of the quantity of the ingredients included in the mixture, and an analysis of the protein, oil, fibre and ash content must be shown.

Pet foods are now being labelled as 'complete' or 'complementary'. A food labelled as a complementary product is not in itself nutritionally complete. Thus a can of dog food indicated as being complementary will need to be served with a biscuit mixer meal, which is also a complementary product, as biscuit mixer served alone would not provide a nutritionally balanced meal either.

The mixer meals, a title which was probably invented to remind users they must be mixed with a meat product to balance the meal, are available in a variety of forms from a very fine puppy grade wholemeal biscuit meal to much larger biscuit chunks suited to larger dogs. Complementary meat products for dogs may be mixed on a half-and-half basis (by weight) with mixer meals to form the complete nutritional repast. Mixer meals may be soaked in hot water or broth – never use boiling liquid – before being mixed with the meat product. Home products, such as stale wholemeal bread or boiled rice, are also complementary 'mixers' and may be used with meat or fish, fresh or canned.

VACUUM-PACKED MEATS

As an alternative to canned meat products for dogs there are several brands of vacuum-packed meats presented in plastic, sausage-like coverings. These are cooked, minced foods and the dogs find them extremely palatable. 'Chubs' is the name given to the sausage packs, though some also are packed in blocks; such packs have certain advantages in that they are easy to open and the wrappings will not fill the garbage cans to overflowing. Chub packs are claimed by their manufacturers to have a good shelf life, but shorter than the shelf life of canned foods. Chubs and vacuum packs in general do not have to be refrigerated before use, but any leftover meat will need to be. These foods are also complementary and should be served with a biscuit mixer. However, new dog foods, or the same types of food in different packs, are continually coming onto the market. Before using any pet food the kennel owner should check the list of contents and directions for use.

DEEP-FROZEN FOOD

Other types of dog food are the deep-frozen products. These may have been cooked and then deep frozen; some are frozen raw and thus need cooking. In either case the water content is quite high and it is necessary to have freezer space for storage, and a good memory so that the frozen blocks are left out to thaw. It is probably useful to have some of these products in the freezer even though it may not be practical to use frozen foods for the entire kennel at all times. Again, frozen foods are complementary products and need a biscuit mixer to complete the menu. Usually, dogs find frozen foods palatable, after they are thoroughly cooked, of course.

BOIL-IN-THE-BAG FOOD

A further method of packing pet foods is in 'boil-in-the-bag' containers, and though these may be favoured by some pet owners, they are not practical for boarding kennel use except, of course, as a tempting starter for a reluctant feeder.

Fresh, canned, vacuum-packed, deep-frozen or boil-in-the-bag meat or fish products for pets which need to be served with a mixer meal are more expensive to use than either the semi-moist complete foods or the complete dry foods, even though boarding kennel owners with larger orders may buy in bulk. They are also more time- and labour-consuming and for these reasons many boarding kennels use complete dry foods for *dogs*; complete canned diets, or fresh foods, are the most suitable for *cats* in the boarding environment, although cats which are used to it may relish a small percentage of dry cat food.

TRIPE

Readers with some experience of dog care will wonder why tripe has not been mentioned among the suitable foods for dogs. Some breeding kennels use tripe, which is satisfactory in protein and fat content but is deficient in minerals. Also, it is not cost-effective. Tripe at its best is purchased direct from the abattoir. The smelly, messy purchase then has to be cleaned, cut and frozen. Unprocessed, it attracts flies. Prepacked, cut or minced tripe can be bought from bulk suppliers, but this is much more expensive and needs freezer space. It is very smelly when defrosting. Tripe can be cooked and, although dogs love it raw, some people insist it should be cooked. Try that and even the dogs may want to leave the premises, not to mention what the neighbours might say. Tripe used consistently in a kennel creates a strong smell which your clients will be quick to notice. It is one ingredient of most manufactured, canned, frozen or vacuum-packed meat foods for dogs, so let them enjoy it in that more innocuous form. Tripe is not a complete food and must be used with a mixer meal.

THE USE OF COMPLETE DRY DIETS FOR DOGS AND CATS

Not a great many pet dogs are fed by their owners on complete dry foods, though the proportion is increasing rapidly now such foods are easily available in supermarkets rather than being largely confined to specialist pet shops. The main reason is the refusal of pet owners to believe that a product which looks like a form of canine breakfast cereal is in fact a complete diet and, of coure, something smelly, moist and meaty is usually more attractive to the dog. Conversely, cat owners are more likely to have used some complete dry cat food. Here the reason is that the complete dry cat foods tend to be packed in smaller amounts, possibly because cats are smaller animals; supermarkets are therefore able to display the products more easily, and they receive a great deal of advertising on television – and most cats eat dry food quite easily.

When deciding to use a complete dry food as a basic kennel diet it is necessary to remember two most important factors. First, as most pet dogs will not be used to such food, they need to be introduced to it gradually, served with a meat product at first, then reducing the meat as the dry food is accepted. Second, dry feeding makes the pet more thirsty, so extra attention must be paid to refilling water bowls and checking that fresh drinking water is always available to each boarder. Particular care must be taken with dogs which continually spill their water bowls, or paddle in them, as some delight in doing. Dry foods can, of course, be fed pre-soaked, though most dogs seem to prefer them to be crunchy rather than mushy – and 'crunchy' is good for keeping teeth and gums clean and in good condition.

Dry feeding has proved to be not only the most convenient but also the most economical and nutritionally satisfactory method of feeding dogs in any environment. Carefully chosen and correctly used dry foods are suitable for all dogs from the puppy to the geriatric stage. Therefore, once a dry complete food has been chosen it can be used as a basic food throughout the entire dog kennel. How will you make your choice of a complete dry food? There are basically three different types, all nutritionally complete. Which is best suited to your kennel requirements? If your choice is governed by price, there is sufficient variation in dry feeding costs to allow for individual choice, and availability of the product must also play a part in the decision. Advertisements for most complete dry foods can be found in the weekly dog papers; the manufacturers' representatives can be seen at championship dog shows, or you can write to the manufacturers for a price-list and the name of the nearest agent, or enquire whether the manufacturer will supply you direct.

In dry dog foods, meat and/or fish meals are added to cooked cereals which are further supplemented with vitamin and mineral additives. The manufacturing method controls the price of these foods, and also the protein content, thus the overall nutritional value.

Dogs, unlike cats, do not require a high-protein diet containing a large proportion of meat. Complete dry foods vary in protein content from about 18 to around 30 per cent. The higher protein content foods are required for bitches in whelp and puppy rearing, and the middle range is nutritionally very suitable for most dogs. Dogs digest cooked cereals well, and also fat from which they get their energy requirements. Vegetables are not important for dogs as they do not require vitamin C. Cereal products also supply fibre and this leads to the formation of a firm stool – a welcome attribute in the boarding kennel environment as cleaning is made easier.

Some complete dry foods may be presented as loose meals, or flaky foods which tend to be low in fat content and are a simple mix of the required ingredients. The flaked cereals are cooked as a rule, and this makes them more digestible. They are best served soaked or mixed with a gravy, and are ready for serving immediately. Many dogs do not find these meals altogether palatable or digestible, so some meat may be added to make them readily acceptable. For these reasons flaked foods are not as readily available as they once were. These foods tend to deteriorate more quickly in storage than other dry foods, but in the boarding kennel environment this is less likely to be a problem as the food turnover is rapid. However, any dry foods you purchase should have a datemark on them: either a date of manufacture, or a 'use by' date.

A second type of dry dog food is pelleted, rather like cattle or pony cubes. These foods tend to be very hard and may be refused by smaller breeds. They do not soak well and usually are less popular, particularly when there are all sizes and ages of dogs to consider. They are also more expensive than the flaky meals.

The most popular type of dry complete diet is the expanded meal. This has a porous texture and the pellets are coated with fat, some brands having a higher oil content than others, though none looks fatty or is greasy to the touch. This meal absorbs liquid easily; therefore expanded meals soak well for the dogs which like a soft mash, and are crispy and crunchy for those which prefer a hard chew.

Though expanded meals are more palatable than either the flaky foods or the rock-hard pellets, nothing is so tasty to a dog as meat. Therefore, while the dog is getting used to his new food the addition of a small amount of canned meat to the expanded meal will help a great deal. Many dogs in breeding kennels are fed on expanded meals and this works well in the boarding kennel too.

Dry, crunchy diets are also good for the dogs' teeth and gums, but do be careful about topping up those water bowls! The manufacturers supply their expanded complete diets with different protein contents and in some cases in different size pellets to cater for all sizes and types of dogs, of all ages and stages of growth and development. Because of the higher protein content of expanded meals – 24 to 30 per cent approximately – a dog needs less of this type of food than if it were fed on the next most popular diet, a half meat and half mixer meal dinner. See the table on page 91, which gives a guide to the food intake requirements of dogs.

The great advantages of complete dry foods are their safety factors: they are nutritious for the pets, very easy and clean to serve, do not attract flies and carry no salmonella risks.

SELF-FEEDING

Sometimes called hopper feeding, this method of feeding the boarders is looked on as the ultimate in time-saving. Another name for the practice is

Daily amount of food

Weight of dog lb	Approx energy need kcal	Mixed diet			Expanded meal oz
		Meal oz	+	Meat oz	
10	425	3½		+3½	4½
20	700	5½		+5½	7½
30	950	7½		+7½	10
40	1200	9½		+9½	12½
50	1400	11		+11	14½
60	1600	13		+13	16½
70	1800	14½		+14½	18½
80	1950	15½		+15½	20½
90	2100	16½		+16½	22
100	2250	18		+18	23½

Reproduced by kind permission of the late Dr Alan Walker and *Kennel and Cattery Management* magazine.

ad lib feeding. Whatever the name used, it consists of filling a hopper or other vessel with a day's supply of dry food for each dog and the feeding chores are done. This method is suitable for use with dry foods because they do not attract flies. Naturally, an adequate water supply also has to be arranged and there are various self-fill drinkers which might be used.

In theory, the dog helps itself to as much food as it wants, when it wants it. The chief disadvantage to *ad lib* feeding is that a great many dogs are greedy and wolf the whole lot at once, which may be quite a shock to the dog's digestive organs. Others scatter the food and play with it. For some boarders the system may work well, but as a rule it is not much favoured in the UK, though it is mentioned more often in the US kennel guides.

An argument against this method of feeding is that pets arriving at your kennel will have come from homes where they are in constant contact with people. They come into what they may look on as a prison, a confined space without the presence of their own humans. The mechanisation of the feeding chores, if mechanisation is not too strong a word, tends to remove another human contact and may not be conducive to easy settling in a strange environment. Furthermore, if two or more dogs from the same household are kennelled together, who will know what dog ate which portion? *Ad lib* feeding has its disadvantages.

CONCLUSION

Expert surveys have shown that the most economical method of feeding dogs overall is to use an expanded complete meal as a basic kennel feed.

It would be extremely wrong to suggest that there should be any 'basic' feed in a cattery, as cats are totally individual and selective in all things.

Economy, though necessary, should not be the overriding factor. The food must be palatable. If the boarders do not like the food, they will not eat it. If the food is not nutritionally adequate and satisfying, they will lose weight and you will have to give them more food – or be accused of starving them! Labour costs and regular food supplies must be considered; it is a nightmare for owners when deliveries are delayed by bad weather or strikes. Obtain all the information you can about the food you think you might like to use in your kennels and find out how to obtain it at the most reasonable prices.

Think carefully about your feeding plans. They play a major part in your care of the boarders. Well-chosen products used to their best advantage can help you over some of the difficulties which, before your initiation as a boarding kennel owner, you may not have realised existed.

8 The Daily Round

Everyday work in a boarding kennel begins early and goes on until it is finished. Much of the work is done during what, in other occupations, are usually called 'unsocial hours'. If you employ staff, they will obviously have set hours. The owners sometimes wonder if they will ever have any time to themselves, particularly in the busy season.

The daily work falls roughly into two major categories which overlap: the first concerns the care of the boarders, keeping their accommodation clean and hygienic, seeing they have exercise and good food and are comfortable and happy; the second concerns the kennel's public face, relationships between the kennel and its human clients, between owner and staff, between the kennel and those who supply its material needs and who give their professional services.

Your clients should be informed through your advertising, brochures, booking application forms and by the largest, clearest sign you can possibly erect at your kennel entrance exactly what hours the kennel is open for business. Or, to put it another way, when your kennel is definitely, absolutely, irrevocably *closed* for business! Because you 'live over the shop', so to speak, clients are often tempted to telephone or visit after normal business hours; it is necessary to guard your privacy – first, because you deserve some time off duty during which you are unavailable to callers, and second, because visitors disturb the dogs and send them into a frenzy of barking, and after-hours disturbances should be avoided if possible. There may be occasions when for a good reason a dog or cat may have to be collected after your official closing time; provided you are given notice of this, arrangements can be made to bring the pet down to the reception area, or to a handy kennel which will not involve disturbing a whole building.

EXERCISE

Pets are used to being let out first thing in the morning, so that is the first task. Let out where? If each kennel has its own attached run, the dogs can be let into their runs while their kennels are cleaned and disinfected, and allowed to return for a biscuit snack or a morning meal if their feeding plan is so arranged.

When kennels do not have their own attached runs it is necessary to take each dog individually to an outside run, and if the weather is wet the dog still has to go out and be dried when it is brought back to its clean kennel. In such establishments it is more helpful if there are a number of medium-sized outdoor exercise runs, all safely fenced of course, rather than one larger area. Dogs should not be mixed together unless they come from the same household; the same applies to cats – those from the same home may share a chalet, otherwise each cat has its own individual unit. Mixing pets from various households is an invitation to fights, something to be avoided at all costs.

Another early morning job, and one which may have to be repeated at suitable intervals throughout the day, is to give special consideration to the new boarders, who may be so well house-trained that they will neither soil their kennel nor perform their toilet functions in the attached run. Such dogs are probably used to the unrestricted use of their gardens at home, or will not foul their own property at all but 'perform' only when taken for walks. Such dogs may respond well to free running in a grass enclosure, in the absence of which it may be necessary to lead-walk the dog. Unfortunately, some pet owners train their dogs rather too well, not understanding that training can be overdone.

Some boarding kennel owners report that cats which have not been used to using a litter tray at home do not take too kindly to one in a kennel. In such cases the problem might be solved by adding some clean earth to the litter tray until the cat has got the message. Needless to say, cat litter trays must be cleaned and disinfected every day.

CLEANING ROUTINE

The subject of kennel cleaning has been dealt with in Chapter 6, but as it is a subject of prime importance it cannot be too heavily emphasised. The basic directions are to clean first, then disinfect using a kennel disinfectant preparation in the exact quantities recommended by the manufacturers. Proper kennel disinfectants are expensive, but necessary; check that the dilutions are measured correctly, not just casually tipped into a bucket.

Though cat boarders are not allowed out of their runs during their stay with you, they too must have their chalets opened each morning and cleaned meticulously according to the recommendations of the Feline Advisory Bureau (see Chapter 6). Cats should always be shut into their chalets at night, with their sanitary tray, and the cat flap secured.

Cleaning includes the proper washing and sterilisation of feeding and drinking bowls. The most intensive floor, wall and run cleaning will be of little use if feeding and drinking vessels are infection carriers; there are special sterilising detergents for these utensils. For cats it may be considered better to use disposable feeding dishes, remembering that many disinfectants are toxic to them. Disposable feeding dishes can be incinerated.

It is useful to have some disinfectant sprays handy in the kennel and cattery. Tego is excellent used in a spray container and is recommended by the Feline Advisory Bureau. Kennel folk can use these sprays to clean their hands after cleaning up vomit or handling a dirty animal. The spray quickly deals with soiled hands and helps to prevent the spread of infection. Small plant misters are ideal for this use.

Newspaper is a very useful commodity in daily use in some kennels and most pets are used to it at home. Not the least of your daily tasks is the disposal of excrement and other kennel rubbish. This has been discussed fully in Chapter 6, but make sure that this is tackled promptly and correctly. There is no worse advertisement for your kennel than to show visitors around uncleaned kennels and runs.

MEALTIMES

When the morning cleaning, tidying and exercising is completed, the boarders may relish either a snack or a meal; it all depends on your catering schedule. Some kennels prefer to serve the main meal in the morning, others in the late afternoon; some owners even prefer to feed the dogs in the late evening; others may decide to feed the dogs two meals a day. When the main meal is planned is not so important as the fact that it is served at the same time every day. A fact which may affect the timing of the dogs' main meal is whether it will be served by you, or your staff. Staff work set hours, and anyone who is off duty at 5 pm is not the person to serve the dogs' main meal at 4.30. Many years ago it was the rule in breeding kennels to fast the dogs on one day each week – this was normally Sunday, the kennel maid's day off. Pet dogs are not used to fasting on one day each week, so regardless of staff problems the dogs are fed one or two meals a day, and cats are fed twice each day.

The approach of feeding time in a dog kennel is noisy. The clatter of food bowls is enough to indicate that a meal is on the way, and joyous anticipatory barking begins. Fortunately, the post-prandial time is quiet and dogs should be allowed to rest after they have eaten. This is when you will need a break too, so make the most of it. Many kennels follow a practice called 'feeding in', which basically means that the dog is brought into its kennel, access to the run is closed, dinner is served and eaten, and only after a rest period is the dog let out again. This prevents the dogs charging around their runs in excitement should something interesting happen right after mealtime, which is not good for the digestion. When they are let out after their rest, the feeding bowls can be collected, washed and sterilised. This is the time to note whether any of the boarders have not eaten their food. Unless a quiet and undisturbed period follows immediately after the food is served, the poor or slow eater may simply be too interested in whatever else is going on and forget they are supposed to be having dinner. Non-eaters should be so indicated on their health charts (see page 100).

THE KENNEL KITCHEN

The kennel kitchen is a very important part of the property. Separate kitchen departments in each kennel block assist in preventing the spread of any infection. Many boarding kennels have a central dog kitchen and, wherever the kitchen is situated, the overriding need is for it to be spotlessly clean and checked daily for hygiene and adequate supplies. A note should be made of any products which need to be re-ordered, and loose meals should be stored in vermin-proof containers. Regardless of whether the basic kennel menu needs any cooking, there should be cooking facilities for special cases and also a refrigerator and a freezer. Such appliances are often available at nominal prices from second-hand shops or auctions, but check that they are in working order before you buy. A washing machine, again a second-hand bargain would do, is a most useful item.

Every kitchen needs a good sink of sufficient size, plus hot and cold water. Those feeding bowls and drinking dishes need to be washed and sterilised and, though the future may bring more automation to this kennel task, the present-day kennel which has even a second-hand automatic dishwasher is in the five-star class. People seeking kennel properties to start their own business frequently report abysmally inadequate kitchen facilities and equipment. Far too many still do not even have a hot water supply, yet these places are inspected and apparently found adequate as the licences are renewed.

Having prepared the boarders' food there is the business of taking the meals to the dogs and cats. In a block of a dozen kennels which has its own kitchen, serving 12 bowls of dinner will not be a daunting task. In a central kitchen serving 60 or 70 meals, the distribution of the food from the kitchen to the eagerly awaiting consumers would tax the ingenuity of an experienced waiter. Some method of transporting as many meals as possible on one journey has to be devised. A trolley seems to be the ideal solution. A water carrier on the trolley allows drinking bowls to be replenished at the same time. Time- and labour-saving devices may be inventions of your own or adapted from other people's ideas. When you look around kennels, note good ideas which you may find useful, or on which you can improve.

BEDS AND TOWELS

The dogs' bedding needs checking every day. It is usually best if the boarders bring their own beds and bedding with them as a reminder of home. Strangely enough, the pets may decide to while away their happy holiday hours in destroying their beds. When a destructive period seems to be approaching it is best to remove the pet's own bedding and substitute some kennel supplies. Alternatively, there are many dogs which, despite their owners having brought their bed and bedding, will prefer to sprawl on the floor of the kennel. For big dogs it is useful to have a large raised bench so they can be encouraged to get up off the floor, preferably onto a blanket. Some large dogs, Great Danes for example, have thin coats and can acquire pressure sores from lying on concrete. Sheets of corrugated cardboard may help 'soften' a hard floor; sometimes carpet outlets will donate out-of-date samples or offcuts to you. All such items, after use as bedding, should be destroyed when the boarder returns home.

Some kennels advertise that they provide 'jumble bedding' – a totally off-putting thought. However, some bedding must be produced. The very hard-wearing, comfortable synthetic fur fabric makes hygienic, washable bedding for dogs and cats. One of its assets is that it does not retain moisture and therefore dries quickly. Blankets are also useful, and special blankets for kennel use may be obtained from the trade stands that appear at championship shows around the country.

Towels are another necessity for use in kennels, but at present there seems to be no specialist supplier of towels for kennel use. Household towels which are past their best usually find their way to the kennel stores; perhaps jumble sales might be another possible source, or auction sales or army surplus sales. One possible solution is to ask the boarders' owners to bring their pets' towels with them, but be sure to send towels home clean! Small dogs with very long coats – Shih Tzu, Lhasa Apsos, Long-haired Dachshunds, Yorkshire Terriers, Pekinese and similar little dogs – can act like wet mops on a rainy day, and must not be allowed to stay wet. A professional electric dog dryer is a great asset in a boarding kennel.

TAKING STOCK

Each day a check needs to be made on the stock of cleaning materials and foodstuffs. Allow time for reordering and delivery, and then allow more time for unexpected delays! Another daily check involves close inspection of run fencing, kennels and cat chalets with a view to possible damage and the need for repairs. Never leave a gate or fence unrepaired. You will undoubtedly be surprised by the damage that may be inflicted by one small pet, or how some dogs can climb chain link fencing, bite through wire netting and generally create chaos. Large dogs simply do a better job more quickly! Latches, hinges, locks, check them all. Some dogs and cats seriously vandalise their accommodation, necessitating ultra-careful cleaning and repairs.

HEATING

A daily check on heating is essential in the interest of comfort and economy. When you take over a boarding kennel or build a new one, you will have little idea at first of the temperature variation within the building. Invest in some maximum–minimum thermometers such as are used in greenhouses. Then keep a note of the highest and lowest temperatures; it will help you to assess heating needs, or in the hottest months show you the degree of heat you and the boarders have to endure. Insulation in kennel building can vary from quite good to non-existent: it affects the running costs of heating appliances in proportion to its effectiveness.

A WORD ABOUT COMPUTERS

The role of computers in the kennel environment was discussed in Chapter 4 and, whatever your IT skills, the paragraph is worth re-reading. Of course, computers are a vital component of modern business, and having a website is essential these days. Computers can be used for many administrative tasks, but this hasn't been without its problems in the case of boarding kennels.There have been many attempts to write a computer program that will cope with the demands of a boarding kennel. Most have not been successful. The reason is that they have usually been based on hotel booking systems that require a relatively simple database, and the relational features, where they have been embedded, have not been able to produce all the reports that even the average kennel requires. First and foremost, humans are all approximately the same size and for that very reason it is easier to create a program that will cope with cats than it is for dogs. Unfortunately, dogs are different sizes, have different temperaments and, crucially, are housed in a variety of different buildings, each of which has its own individual characteristics. Cat chalets are pretty standard and you can have several blocks labelled A, B, C, etc and, usually, any cat can go into any one. It is just not the same with dogs. As the kennels you are going to buy expanded, new blocks were added with different designs and made of different materials. Block A might have 8 kennels for small dogs, 10 kennels for medium dogs and 4 kennels for large dogs. Another block might have a specially built 'family' kennel for owners who have three or four dogs and who like them to be kept together, plus an assortment of irregular-sized kennels, some with runs and some pens from which the dogs have to be taken out for exercise. Then there are the converted pig pens, due for demolition within five years under the MLCs agreement but still being used for the strays that the kennel has been contracted to house for the local dog warden. A computer program that can handle this sort of diversity (and computers are designed to handle lots of very similar calculations) is not easy to write to begin with. Then, to make it worthwhile, report functions for different feeding regimes for each dog, their medication, their medical history and their individual characteristics (afraid of large black dogs – keep away) and you begin to see the difficulties involved.

The best program in the experience of the author does not even try to allocate pets to individual kennels. Where a computer can score is in the diary and the current and future occupancy. As pets are being booked in for particular periods it can warn you if you are close to capacity. However, bearing in mind the different sizes of kennels, you will have to manually sort the records to allocate sizes of dogs to the kennels available (but you probably have to do this anyway if you are using a paper-based system). What you really need to know in June is that for August you are full for large dogs, but you have room for three medium and six small ones.

The facility to print individual record cards for each pet is useful. Under MLC guidelines, this information should be available at the point of care, usually posted on the door of the kennel so that staff are aware of all the animal's details. One problem is that even after you have posted all your existing clients into the program, putting in new clients takes time. With a paper-based system you can book new clients into a diary and then ask them to fill in a record card with all their details while you deal with a new customer. Using a computer, you have to do all that yourself. This may not matter if they turn up on a quiet Thursday morning, but it can be frustrating for anyone waiting to get off to catch their train or plane on a busy Friday afternoon.

To end on a positive note, a computer program can print out your conditions and a contract for clients to sign (it is still a requirement of the 1963 Act that this is obtained) and invoices. This last facility saves a lot of calculation. The Chilworth Kennels and Cattery Management Programme, which does allow you to allocate kennel type/size and even includes a graphing facility that assists with early identification of occupational 'peaks', can be obtained from Christopher Armstrong, Chilworth Kennels and Cattery, Lordswood Lane, Chilworth, Southampton SO16 7JG (tel: 023 8076 6876;www.chilworth kennels.com.

HEALTH RECORD CARDS

Each boarder should have its own health record card updated daily while it stays with you. Even in a small kennel it is no use relying solely on your memory of what has happened during the course of each day. The boarder's health card can be hung in its kennel, out of reach of the pet, and should record basic details such as normal bowel movements, or otherwise, diarrhoea, constipation, vomiting, lameness, runny eyes, a cough, whether a bitch is in season, or anything which seems unusual. Cats are more inclined to suffer in silence and particular care should be paid to them. Whether or not the cat is eating should be noted, also if a cat has difficulty in urinating: this is a situation that may need prompt veterinary attention. The owner should check the pet's health records daily, and if there is any concern, request a visit from the vet. Therefore, do not leave the daily health check until late afternoon; vets are busy people too and have to plan their rounds. Without a written health record it would be difficult to answer the basic questions the vet will have to ask in order to help in diagnosis.

A continuity of care is essential in the boarding kennel and cattery, and as the same staff may not be on duty all the time the health cards provide that essential continuity. Record cards can be designed to suit your own needs, just as long as you and your staff understand your system and use it correctly.

GROOMING

Dogs and cats in boarding kennels should be groomed regularly, and particularly before leaving. Whether you offer only simple basic grooming (that is, brushing and combing with a good-quality coat spray dressing), or whether you have a trained canine beautician and can therefore offer full bathing, grooming and trimming facilities for all breeds, is a matter you should make clear to your clients. The basic brushing, combing and tidying with the help of a pleasant-smelling coat dressing should be part of the normal service. The full, professional treatment is an extra. However, no dog should leave your kennels looking unkempt. Check carefully the coats of all long- or heavy-coated breeds which may board with you. It is quite likely that you will find many are badly matted, and if you do not offer a full grooming service you should suggest that the dogs should be taken to a professional beautician, preferably a member of the Pet Care Trust, for the correct coat treatment. A matted dog is often a miserable dog, and very uncomfortable.

RECEPTION AREA

The daily round will bring visitors to your kennel: people bringing or collecting boarders, merchandise deliverymen, people who wish to inspect your kennels before making a firm booking, local government officials inspecting your kennels under statutory regulations and almost anybody you are prepared to admit. Visitors will interest the dogs if they see them arrive, or if they can watch the cars come and go. Dogs show their interest with a vocal greeting. If your visitors' arrivals and your reception area can be screened from the boarders' view, so much the better, and if visitors are restricted to your official opening hours the dogs should be quieter in the evenings. Prospective clients who want to look around the kennel should be invited at certain times only, and adults rather than children encouraged. Of course, people should see where their pets are going to stay, but you are not providing kennel tours for fun, so plan these visits for midweek if possible. At the weekends you are likely to be extra busy and possibly short of staff.

Security dictates that entrance to your kennel should be on admittance by one of the staff. People arriving need to know what to do; place a notice on the gate asking visitors to ring the bell and wait, but make sure the bell is connected and answered without delay. There is nothing more demoralising for a person who may be rather reluctantly boarding a pet than to arrive at your kennel and find nobody waiting with a friendly word of welcome. It also gives a very poor impression of your kennel's security! The sign reading, 'RECEPTION. PLEASE RING AND WAIT' is a much better start.

The reception room may also be the kennel office. It is advisable to keep all the bookwork in one place or you will be forever wanting to refer to something which is in another place when needed. How you organise your office work may depend on whether you or your partner have any experience of secretarial work, or whether you are going to employ some part-time clerical help. Under the Animal Boarding Establishments Act 1963 you are bound to keep a register of the animals boarded with you. Keep your boarders' register in your reception area; basically, it should show which dogs are in which kennels, when they arrived and when they are expected to depart. Advance bookings can be entered in pencil until confirmation and a deposit is received; then the booking can be inked in. Never overbook the accommodation as there is always the possibility that an owner may be quite legitimately delayed and unable to collect a pet on time.

You will also need a file in which to keep the booking forms, which are a business contract between you and the pet owner. Booking forms should always be issued in duplicate; one copy for your file, and the other copy for the pet owner – both copies showing clear signatures. Your kennel stationery and brochures need to be in your office and reception room, also the typewriter or computer if you have one and, as you will be taking money, a lockable compartment or safe, depending on the size of your business and what valuables must be secured. It is sensible to empty both safe and till regularly so that cash, cheques and credit card receipts are kept safe. Kennels are busy and it is all too easy to leave the reception area unattended. Even charity collection boxes have been stolen from reception areas. The reception office should be clean, neat and comfortable in its own way, and as attractive as possible, as this will be your clients' first introduction to your premises. There should be a spare cat-carrying basket in case someone arrives with puss loose in the car. A large dog crate is also a useful item to have handy, and some spare slip leads. The reception area should look efficient and inviting. Shabby paint and an air of dilapidation can be remedied fairly easily, and a few doggy pictures, prize rosettes, or even attractive pot plants give a welcoming appearance.

The telephone should be in the office of course, though you may have extensions at other strategic points. Some people still do not like answering machines or voicemail, so make sure they are personalised, give an emergency number in case of genuine need and clearly state your opening times. Digital cordless telephones or mobile phones which can be carried around with you are of course a great option.

One very important item which should be kept in your reception office and updated each year is a list of canine breed rescue societies and the names of the people responsible for administering them for each breed. You can get a copy, free, from The Kennel Club, 1 Clarges Street, Piccadilly, London W1J 8AB (tel: 0870 606 6750; www.thekennelclub.org.uk). If owners of uncollected boarders are impossible to trace after a period, the kennel owner usually tries to re-home a healthy animal and often the breed rescue society can help. Alternatively, if a client mentions that he or she is hoping to find another home for the dog, the kennel owners may put the person in touch with the breed rescue society direct and save themselves a headache! Another address to note is that of Cats Protection, National Cat Centre, Chelwood Gate, Haywards Heath, Sussex, RH17 7TT (tel: 08707 708 649; www.catsorg.uk).

ARRIVALS AND DEPARTURES

When new boarders arrive, check their booking forms with the owners and note that they have been signed by them and by you, or by someone signing with your authority. Confirm that the pet owners understand the terms of boarding and check carefully the pets' vaccination certificates. *No boarder can be admitted without evidence of full vaccination for PvDHL plus any booster or kennel cough vaccination the animal requires.* (Note the advice on pages 75–77.) This is not only sensible on your part but is a requirement of many local councils. Make sure you have the owner's correct address, the name of their veterinary surgeon, and a contact with whom you can get in touch if necessary, and check that the owners know exactly when they are due to collect their pets. All these checks are very important. There have been numerous occasions when a pet's owner has had to be contacted and the kennel staff have been told that the person moved house several years ago.

New boarders must be seen safely to their holiday kennel or chalet. It is easier for you to use your own leads. Strong nylon slip leads are easy to use and can be carried in your pocket. Choke chains should be used with care and assistants instructed in their correct use. Cats should be taken to their chalets in their baskets and not released until they are safely within their own enclosure and the door is firmly shut. Remind kennel staff to be just as welcoming to the pets as they are to the owners, and to be prepared to give the new arrivals a little extra attention to help them settle down.

Of course, no dog leaves your boarding kennel unless the bill is paid in full. No money, no pet. Bank cards guarantee cheques up to £50 or £250 in some cases. Over that amount, it is trust, debit, credit card or cash. At the departure stage it will be a great relief to all concerned if no unexpected extras are added to the bill; a charge for veterinary treatment is one possibility, but that may never occur if your kennels are fully covered by insurance with one of the major canine insurance companies such as Pet Plan.

Another facet of the daily round is whether or not you will collect or deliver boarders. There are two major considerations here. People should always be able to see where their pets are going to stay, which means they should visit your kennels, and collecting and delivering take time – time is money and there are petrol costs and the wear and tear on your car or van. On the other hand, it is an added value service you can charge for. However, for small kennels it is better if the owners of the pets do the fetching and carrying, but there will be some instances when flexibility in this matter will pay dividends. Somebody's car has broken down, perhaps, or some other hitch in the plans makes it impossible for them to transport Rover to your kennels. Help them out; make a charge or, in certain cases, you may be prepared to waive the collection charge. Use your discretion.

ENQUIRIES

Almost every day prospective clients, or other inquisitive folk, telephone or e-mail to ask how much you charge to board dogs or cats. Try to work out a plan for answering such calls or e-mails, and train your staff to use whatever method you have worked out. Boarding kennel owners have to be their own salesman, and though they can hardly put a foot in the door, they can perhaps mention some useful, attractive and enticing information in response to an enquiry. It takes only a few seconds to give some information, or obtain some, *before* you tell the price! Answer the question, 'How much do you charge?' with 'What sort of dog/cat do you have?' Whatever size, breed, etc is mentioned will be your favourite, and you have exactly the right accommodation for them. Of course you will go on to say that your prices are inclusive of all the pets' needs, heating, insurance and, if necessary, veterinary fees. In short you are offering absolutely super value in ideal surroundings at £X per day or whatever the relevant fee may be. There is nothing wrong with a good line of salesmanship, the point of which is to instil confidence in the mind of the potential customer and, without saying so, make it quite clear that the cheapest is not always the best. You are running a business which must be profitable despite the weird ideas that some people have about it being not quite the thing to make money out of a doggy pursuit. You are offering a service – a good one; if it does not pay, the service is lost to the neighbourhood and your business is lost too.

PROBLEMS WHICH MAY BE ENCOUNTERED

Aged pets

Elderly canines and felines may sometimes have to become boarders. If they have not been regularly boarded over the years, it may be a very great shock to them and have the direst consequences. Warn the owners that it is a terrible strain on the older dog or cat and show these boarders every attention and extra comfort – which may include smaller meals and more often – and the quietest kennel available so that the dog will not be disturbed too much. Conversely, the aged feline may relish its own secluded chalet, with all its needs cared for, meals-on-wheels, and extra fuss, and be very content. If an elderly boarder is having any medicines, make sure you have an adequate supply for its stay with you, and be sure to give the drugs as directed.

Some kennels will not accept older pets. This is a shame – much better to ensure that their special needs are catered for (for which an increased charge can be made).

Bitches in season

Always ask the pet owners if a bitch is spayed, or when she is due in season. If a bitch has not been spayed, it is quite likely that the experience of coming into the boarding kennel may bring her into season, or she may already be on heat and that is why her owners have boarded her with you. A bitch in season will delight, tease and annoy the dogs, even though she does nothing special to attract their attention. The boys will *know*! Put her in a kennel and run which does not have a male neighbour on either side. Remember that a determined male can be a Houdini plus and will attempt to join her. Secure, covered runs help a great deal, but accidental marriages have occurred. Should you be so lax, you must stand the cost of the annulment: an injection given by the vet. A disadvantage of bitches in season is that the dogs love to serenade them, preferably about 1 am!

Fights

To be avoided at all costs. Make it clear to your clients that all dogs arrive at the kennels on a lead, and that cats are securely shut into their baskets or cat carriers. Cats are not let out of their carriers until safely within their own quarters with the run door firmly closed. Dogs are moved from A to B within the kennel on a slip lead and only pets from the same household are allowed to be kennelled together or play together in an exercise run. Even then it is wise to have written permission. A dog in the boarding environment, though quite amiable and docile, may be cherishing a desire to have a go at its neighbour or the dog up the corridor, and once the opportunity for a punch-up occurs the results can be serious; in such circumstances the human is very likely to be bitten and the dogs may bite each other badly too. Do *not* let fights start.

Fleas

Some boarding kennels make it a practice to spray every new boarder on arrival with Frontline or one of the other prescribed flea killers, just to be on the safe side. If you have the facilities and the expertise for bathing and grooming, a flea bath could well be indicated: use a veterinary prescribed shampoo such as Quellada or Derasect or one recommended by your vet.

Kennel cough

Any coughing dog should be considered with suspicion, as kennel cough is very infectious and by the time you have heard the first coughs and splutters the dog will have passed it on to most of its fellow boarders. Some dogs are not severely affected by kennel cough, though it makes others very ill. Those most susceptible are the very young and the very old, or any dog whose health is somewhat below par. The outbreak may start with a dog which was perfectly well when it arrived but was incubating the disease; other dogs may go home apparently well and start coughing in a day or two. Veterinary advice should be sought as there may be secondary problems; antibiotics and a cough syrup may be prescribed. Remember that dogs which have recovered from kennel cough remain infectious for several months, so suggest that your clients consult their vet regarding protection with Intrac nasal vaccine before boarding.

Medicines

The kennel owner, or a person of responsibility and experience only, should administer prescribed medicine according to instructions, and each dose should be recorded on the pet's health record card. This is not a job for junior staff or part-timers. A tranquilliser which calms down one dog may not affect the next. A pill which has no effect on a small dog may knock out a larger breed for many hours. Tolerance of tranquillisers and certain other drugs appears to vary, not only with the size of the dog but also with the breed. Not all dogs react alike to medicines.

Worms

It is possible that you may see roundworms, which look like thin spaghetti, or even tapeworm segments, which look like particles of long-grain rice, in a dog's motions or in the anal area. If so, do not rush in with the worm medicine until you have checked with your vet that you have the right anthelmintic (worm medicine). Should a cat produce worms, *do not* use your dog worming medicine! Cat medicines are not the same as dog medicines. Follow the directions carefully.

Tail damage

A large dog with a very waggy tail may damage its tail tip against kennel walls or run partitions; then every wag sprays a shower of blood spots which inevitably worries the dog's owner, the kennel owner and the staff far more than it bothers the dog. I have no figures yet but it seems likely that this will become a greater problem in the future now that dogs' tails may no longer be docked. Tail damage of this sort is to be avoided if possible. A very excitable dog which likes to jump up with a woof and a wag at every opportunity may be calmed down if it is put in a quieter kennel where it cannot see quite so much of what is going on. Never resort to tranquillisers without specific advice.

Post-mortems

If one of your boarders dies while in your care, an event one always hopes will not happen but which unfortunately can occur through no fault of yours, your vet should always be asked to ascertain the cause of death. This may involve a post-mortem, and certainly will involve your insurance company: another reason why you need proper insurance coverage organised by a specialist company. You cannot afford legal claims for reimbursement, nor ill-will from a bereaved client. For a client to return from a wonderful holiday only to find a beloved pet has died is a truly harrowing experience. The only thing worse is to be the person who has to tell them!

The Animal Care College runs a course on handling pet bereavement. You may find this useful if you are inexperienced or you have staff who are expected to deal with everything if you are away.

Noise

Last, but by no means least, is the most common kennel problem of all – noise. Noise is the chief reason for complaints against a kennel, and complaints are always worrying. Everything else about your establishment may be perfect, but anyone who is annoyed by the barking will not see one good point in your favour.

Your environmental health officer will be the person instructed to visit you if there are complaints of noise, and may well have some helpful suggestions to make for alleviating the problem. Well-insulated buildings will deaden the sound of barking from within. Restricting visitors to certain times, not accepting or releasing boarders after 6 pm, feeding late and in the afternoon and generally finishing all kennel work by early evening is helpful. The kennel which has visitors coming and going at all hours is bound to provide sufficient disturbances to keep the dogs noisy. Apart from annoying the neighbours, it is not a good idea to allow unwanted barking; the dogs go home with hoarse voices and sore throats!

Sometimes it is necessary to do some detective work to find out why there is unusual noise. For example, at night some kennels use infra-red overhead heaters, of which there are two types: one gives a warm red glow of light as well as heat, and the other is known as a dull emitter and gives comforting warmth but no light. Use only the dull emitter type of infra-red heater or the pet may wake up and bark because somebody has left the light on! They feel disorientated, and say so.

VETERINARY SURGEONS' VISITS

If it is necessary to call a veterinary surgeon to visit a boarder, try to contact the practice as early as possible in the day – a good reason for an early morning health check in the kennel. But illness can occur at any time of the day or night and attention sought as soon as possible is the best plan.

If you can take the animal to the veterinary surgery, treatment tends to be quicker and less expensive, but this is often impossible. Consider how veterinary examinations can best be carried out at your kennel before the need arises. Will the vet see the patient in its own kennel? Is the kennel big enough? Is it sufficiently well lit to allow a proper examination? Do you have a dispensary, or treatment/grooming room which you could use for such visits? Is there a sink? Is your boarders' first aid box well stocked? If a cat needs to be examined, this is best done in the cat's own chalet. The FAB-suggested individual chalet has a bench underneath the window and a light, and allows two people to be present while a cat is examined. Penthouse cat accommodation is quite difficult in such circumstances, and some forms of cat accommodation are totally inadequate yet somehow they have still been licensed. If it is impossible to examine a cat in its own accommodation, moving it may increase the chance of spreading infection.

Isolation

By law you must provide one isolation section for dogs and one for cats if you board both genera. It would be extremely cruel to expect an ailing cat to be comfortable and reassured if its isolation quarters were in close proximity to the dogs' sick quarters. For either genus the isolation unit must be adequate in size, comfortable, with provision for extra heating – an overhead infra-red dull emitter thermostatically controlled would be suitable – and the units should be in a place where you and your staff can easily give the extra attention which will be needed.

Many kennel proprietors argue that they do not need isolation facilities because if a pet is infectious it is at their veterinary surgery. Some Environmental Services Officers have accepted this, but you should check.

Medication

Finally, if you do not know the easy ways to give medicines to cats or dogs when they are prescribed, ask your vet to show you. Many dogs will take a pill concealed in a piece of meat, hidden in a titbit of cheese or pilchard perhaps. Liquid medicine is easiest given from a syringe; ask your vet for one. Giving a pill to a cat may need a step-by-step lesson from an expert. Have somebody show you and thus avoid some scratches! A few pet animals are 'unpillable'; no matter what ruse you try the pill will not stay down. In such cases the medicine can perhaps be obtained in a liquid form. If medicine cannot be given orally, injection may be the answer. Never give up; if a sick animal requires medication, then it is your duty to see that the dose goes in, one way or another, and reducing yourself to a shaking wreck will not help matters.

FINAL CHECK

The kennel owner's last duty of the day is to make a final round of the kennel property and check that all boarders are in their kennels, or cat units, and appear to be well. Check that all buildings are secure and that the outside runs have been left absolutely clean. Then it is 'lights out' after a busy, satisfying and, hopefully, not too difficult day.

9 Kennel Staff

In the early days of your boarding kennel ownership you may find that your kennel can be managed without extra help. A husband-and-wife team, or two working partners, can usually manage very well in a small business, but the single-handed kennel owner will need some back-up help if only of a part-time nature. There are so many things which only the owner can attend to, and the basic kennel work has to be done regardless of interruptions. Some of the enjoyment of being your own boss begins to wear thin if you are constantly overtired through attending single-handed to all the cleaning, maintenance, bookwork and queries from clients, prospective clients and officials of one sort of another.

Before employing help, decide if kennel help is what you need; that is, do you need help with the actual care of the kennels and the dogs and cats? You might find that you and your partner are very happy doing everything in the animal departments but that outside help with the housework, garden, children or secretarial work is what you really want. Kennel work is demanding and strenuous and therefore meals need to be more than a rushed snack when you can get around to it, or a take-away evening meal from whatever local source is available. You will need time out to visit the dentist, have a hair-cut or attend to any of the small necessities of life. Perhaps regular full- or part-time help is needed, but not actually with the animals. Boarding kennel owners who are also active in the dog or cat exhibition world, and wish to remain so, will find that they need experienced help with the boarders as they may have to leave them in charge of an assistant who will have full responsibility in their absence. Ancillary help is one end of the staff spectrum; a kennel manager/

manageress is at the other. Determine your own particular needs and also what you can afford to pay. There is sure to be a going rate for domestic/ garden/office work in your area, and there are many people seeking work of this kind. Working in the actual kennels tends to be low paid, and although there are many applicants for such jobs, finding suitable people to work with animals may not be quite so easy.

Maybe your predecessor employed staff who might wish to stay on and work for you. This can be very useful in the early days as you will have someone with local knowledge, and as long as there is an understanding that when you are the owner your methods must be followed, the takeover period may be considerably eased.

If you feel that you can manage very well but would find an extra pair of hands useful at the busiest times, namely weekends and holiday periods, contact the careers teacher at your local secondary school. There are many reliable youngsters who want to work with animals and need a weekend and holiday job. Sort out the applicants who still want to work in kennels once they understand all that it entails and you may find yourself a helper of considerable worth. Many a veterinary surgeon or veterinary nurse fostered the germ of a career with animals by working at the local boarding kennels during school holidays.

ACCOMMODATION

Daily workers or part-timers will need no accommodation other than decent washing and toilet facilities, plus of course somewhere to relax for a few minutes with a morning coffee or afternoon cup of tea; it is surprising how many kennels fail in this basic aspect of staff comfort though their licence insists they provide such facilities. If accommodation has to be provided for living-in staff, consider whether you would like to live in it before expecting anyone else to accept it. Many kennels provide caravan accommodation, which can be palatial but more often is anything but. Whether this is satisfactory depends on many things. While there are many people wanting to work in kennels, a lot of them would not be able to tolerate sub-standard accommodation, which in any case they should not be offered. Kennels which provide excellent accommodation keep their staff. It is not fair to expect resident staff to live in squalor, and this can be seen at some kennels, knowing they would hate to leave their jobs because they really care for the boarders and their work. Without decent accommodation, how can the staff have decent food? Without good, well-balanced meals, hard physical work is very hard indeed. A conscientious employer will think of the health and well-being of his or her staff as well as the health and comfort of the boarders. Of course, as an employer you also have a duty to comply with health and safety law. For more information see www.hse.gov.uk or telephone 0845 3450055.

Sometimes kennel positions are advertised to 'live as family'. This is often a very satisfactory state of affairs, with the employee's keep being deducted from the overall wage. However, care must be taken in selecting such staff, as whoever lives in the house needs to be able to get along happily with all other members of the household. When this sort of situation works it is one of the best possible arrangements. There must be a 'happy family' feeling about the whole kennel whether staff live in or out, with consideration shown on both sides.

STAFF TRAINING

Having chosen a new employee, you will have to provide some training and have some rules, whether your helper is to work part- or full-time and regardless of whether he or she has worked in a kennel previously.

Security is the first subject you must impress upon your staff, in whatever capacity they work. They must always close gates and doors, and ensure that they are firmly latched to prevent escapes.

New recruits should be instructed in the correct methods of kennel cleaning and the basic daily routine. Learning to be an efficient kennel assistant is not achieved in one short, easy lesson: the daily routine of cleaning, exercising and feeding is only part of the job. It is equally important for kennel staff to be trained to be observant, to think for themselves, to watch and enjoy dogs and cats – however many years one works with animals, there will always be something different. Choose your kennel staff carefully and train them well. Procedure sheets for each process are a valuable reference tool and writing them (preferably with your staff) can be a very useful exercise.

Staff should be taught how to deal with clients in the best interests of all concerned. This means a friendly greeting whether in person or answering the telephone. It is more welcoming to answer the phone with 'Beerode Kennels, may I help you?' than simply by saying 'Hello', or even 'Beerode 4321'. When meeting a client, staff should address them by name and ask the pet's name – and remember it! Similarly, staff badges with a name on them – just 'Sally', 'Jimmy' or 'Jane' – are sufficient to help clients remember to whom they were talking. People often feel quite unsure about bringing their pets to a boarding kennel; if they find a friendly service, their own confidence in your establishment is boosted.

Above all, remind your staff that no matter what toil, struggle or irritation any day may bring, kindness to the animals is paramount. The boarders' health, welfare, needs and comforts must always come first.

Some uniformity of clothing for kennel staff is smart and eye catching. There is nothing wrong with jeans, but patched, frayed or dirty jeans or slacks should not be tolerated. Even a simple T-shirt with the kennel name or logo overprinted would be attractive, or perhaps a tabard overall.

Footwear needs to be clean and sturdy; wellington boots are the universal kennel footwear for much of the time but there is no need for them to look as though they have never been washed.

If you are interested in improving the professional image of the boarding kennel business, you may wish to contact the Animal Care College for details of their kennel staff training courses. The course provides some theoretical back-up for students who are receiving practical training at kennels and other animal care establishments. The college provides a wide range of courses in animal care, including one for kennel managers and proprietors.

CHECKING-IN

Kennel staff should be the ones to take the new arrivals to their holiday accommodation, settle them into the kennel or cat chalet, make a little fuss of them – and return fairly soon to remind them they have not been forgotten. During the pet's visit it needs some tender loving care and kind words as well as an absolutely clean kennel and excellent food plus enjoyable exercise. Kennel staff should also be able to attend to basic grooming during the stay.

Continuity of care is most important in the boarding kennel complex. The boarders are used to one person, mainly, caring for them at home and prefer to relate to one person; in your kennels the cat or dog will, albeit gradually, accept its kennel assistant as 'Mum' or 'Dad' for the duration. Continuity is therefore an important psychological aspect of care. It is also an important physical aspect, for the kennel staff who regularly attend to a group of animals may instinctively, or can be trained to, notice small irregularities which might be the forerunners of major problems.

INCOME TAX AND NATIONAL INSURANCE

An employer is responsible for deducting income tax from his or her employees' pay, and non-collection can incur penalties. A free booklet, *Employer's Guide to PAYE*, is available from your local tax office, which will also supply you with deduction cards and code tables. The money deducted is paid to the tax office monthly, together with National Insurance contributions.

National Insurance deduction tables are provided by the Department for Work and Pensions. The employer is responsible for deducting a monthly contribution from any employee earning more than a fixed amount a week and also to *make* a payment in respect of each employee.

Kennel work is one of the lower paid jobs and in many cases the kennel assistant's wage (or training allowance) is below the statutory amount requiring the employer to pay National Insurance contributions. Low-paid staff should be aware that they may pay a voluntary NI contribution, but that it would be more beneficial to pay a self-employed category contribution, which is only a few pence higher, as this would entitle them to sickness benefits should the need arise. A visit to the local offices of the Department for Work and Pensions would provide you, and your staff, with all the relevant information.

CONTRACT OF EMPLOYMENT

Each employee must receive a contract of employment (which can be in the form of a letter) setting out:

- job title;
- the rate of pay, and whether it is paid weekly or monthly;
- normal hours of work;
- holidays and holiday pay;
- provision for sick pay;
- pension and pension schemes;
- notice required by both parties;
- any disciplinary rules relating to the job;
- grievance procedures.

An itemised pay statement must be handed over with the pay giving:

- gross wages;
- net wages;
- deductions and the reasons for them;
- details of any other payments.

Employment contracts and employee rights are becoming increasingly complicated, and it is recommended that you take legal advice. The small business service www.businesslink.gov.uk is a good place to start.

HEALTH HAZARDS

Employers should ensure that kennel staff are inoculated against tetanus and that they receive boosters if necessary. Everyone who works in kennels should be covered by accident insurance which should be an intergrated part of your business cover, and employers should check that working conditions comply with the terms of the Health and Safety at Work Act 1974 and subsequent orders.

Certain people who work with animals may be considered as being at risk from rabies; employees at quarantine kennels come into this category and in such cases vaccination against rabies is available to them. Such vaccinations are not available through the National Health Service and are quite expensive. Consult your doctor on this matter or the Vaccinating Centre, 53 Great Cumberland Place, London W1 7LH (tel: 020 7262 6456).

With the opening of the Eurotunnel in 1993 there is some concern that the danger of rabies occurring in Britain has been increased. Though we are assured that strict precautions are taken on both sides of the English Channel, Eurotunnel appeared to present an extra route for the greatest danger of all – the smuggling of pets into Britain. However, changes in the law that have been implemented by the adoption of the Pet Travel Scheme (usually referred to as the Pet Passport) have greatly increased the canine and feline traffic into and out of the UK by boat and plane as well as the Eurotunnel train. The danger from rabies remains, of course, and entry by animals from countries not covered by the legislation and by those that do not fulfil the PTS criteria is still illegal as well as dangerous.

It is essential that any suspicions of the illegal entry of dogs, cats or other small animals be reported to the authorities, and vigilance by knowledge-able people in the kennel business will be of vital importance. We must keep rabies out of Britain!

10 Kennel Buildings

The standard work on kennel buildings is *Essential Kennel Design* by David Key, available through the Our Dogs Bookshop (www.ourdogs.co.uk). This is an extensive and detailed book and is highly recommended. David has kindly allowed me to use many of the drawings from his excellent book.

It is the kennel owners and their staff who make the boarding kennel popular and profitable, and the best kennel buildings in the world cannot compensate for inefficient management and an unpleasant manner. However, when you, as a prospective purchaser, visit a kennel which is being offered for sale, what makes the biggest impact on your mind is the first sight of the kennel property! What do you think your future clients will notice first? The outside runs and larger exercise areas or garden which meet the eye and are noted for their safety and attractive appearance, or their shabbiness, plethora of weeds and the reek of powerful disinfectant? Good disinfection need not involve strong or unpleasant odours. Safe, secure buildings need not resemble a prison.

Boarding kennel proprietors report that many people telephone to ask details of fees, but those who can be persuaded to visit a well-situated and visually attractive kennel usually make firm bookings. Appearances obviously count for a great deal, though we know good management must run alongside if the appearance is not to be 'skin deep'.

Kennel and Cattery Design
Full page colour

Kennel and Cattery Design
Full page edit

ADAPTING EXISTING PROPERTY

If you see a property which you consider sub-standard, but which you feel you could improve easily, check first with the local authority to find out whether certain stipulated improvements have been recommended and whether or not you would be able to implement the council's requirements. It is possible that in some cases a district authority may allow improvements to be phased in gradually. Kennel owners who have been able to purchase what are apparently ideal kennels invariably find that there are still some improvements they wish to make.

Old pig sties or other farm buildings may have been converted into dog accommodation, sometimes with fairly satisfactory results. In other cases unfitted buildings have been converted into kennelling with the use of purpose-made galvanised mesh, solid galvanised sheet panels or partitioning. Various firms make galvanised kennel panelling, either mesh or solid, for indoor or outdoor use; set on levellers on good concrete flooring, individual panels may be built up into any appropriate number of units, and in a suitable building are a very adequate form of kennelling but may not fulfil the requirements of the Model Licence Conditions.

Beware of the small cage accommodation too frequently offered to cats. Certain indoor catteries, as described in the Feline Advisory Bureau's own guide, are perfectly suitable for boarding, but any barn with a pile of cages described as a boarding cattery, or 'caravan used as cattery' as sometimes seen in advertisements, should be viewed with suspicion. In such cramped accommodation the risk of infection is great enough to endanger the animals' health and thus be a threat to your business and is quite unacceptable. Converted kennel accommodation usually depends on there being several securely fenced large outdoor exercise runs to which the boarders are taken individually several times a day as each kennel may not have the recommended adjoining run. Some boarding kennels advertise that all dogs are walked individually on leads every day, possibly because there is no securely fenced free outside exercise area. This can work well in a small kennel provided the owners are conscientious and can make time for it. Having to walk boarders on public roads because of lack of exercising areas within a kennel property is a security risk and is not recommended.

NEW DESIGNS

New designs in kennel buildings are coming into use and it is well worth visiting such places as the Wood Green Animal Shelters, where circular buildings are proving highly satisfactory. For information, contact Wood Green Animal Shelters (tel: 08701 904090; www.woodgreen.org.uk).

Blue Cross and Dogs Trust have some of the most advanced and best-designed kennels. The newer ones are 'state of the art' and very expensive to construct but are worth visiting for ideas. For lists of centres, see www.dogstrust.org.uk and www.bluecross.org.uk.

A list of quarantine kennels may be obtained from the Department for Environment, Food and Rural Affairs (Animal Health Division, tel: 020 8330 4411). Visits to quarantine kennels are strictly by appointment only, but seeing several will show you that designs vary, though all must work within Defra regulations.

CONVENTIONAL KENNEL ACCOMMODATION

The recommended type of kennel accommodation will have attached runs. These designs fall into four main types:

1. an interior corridor with kennels on one side only, each kennel leading through to an individual run;
2. a central corridor with kennels on either side, each kennel leading to its individual run – the most satisfactory type generally, as the dogs can see friends across the aisle;
3. kennel compartments with a run attached, access being through the run to the kennel, so that once the dog is shut in at night it might as well be shut in a large cupboard or coal bunker, as it has no contact with, or view of, any other dog;
4. purpose-built kennel units with a central corridor, but instead of bars or mesh there are solid doors and partitions on each side of the corridor – although this plan may reduce noise, as the dogs cannot see into the central corridor, neither can the kennel staff see the dogs.

Generally speaking, the second type of corridor kennels is the easiest to manage, cheapest to build from scratch, and the most appreciated by the pets. Many have the access hatch to the run area opened both from outside the run gate and from inside the corridor. Cleaning of inside kennels when the dogs are in the runs is easy, and when the inside cleaning and disinfecting is over it is a simple matter to attend to the outside runs. Incidentally, few architects or builders understand the extent of the 'fall' required in a kennel run. It should be a real slope, otherwise puddles occur and dogs may become unwell.

Outside runs attached to kennels are most satisfactory if they are separated from each other by 1-metre-high solid walls topped with galvanised mesh panels to give a 2-metre-high division. Such compartments are the easiest to keep clean. Runs may be partially covered to provide shelter, or fully mesh covered to deter the fence-climbing escape artists. When choosing mesh gates always check the fastenings for firm closing. Clever dogs can work out ways of opening anything which is not absolutely paw proof.

In addition to security within the kennel buildings, the boarding kennel owner must also secure the property against intruders. This means secure perimeter fencing and locked gates after business hours. It also means that your property should not be left unattended. Dogs and puppies have been stolen from boarding kennels, so when thinking of security, remember it is a two-way problem.

The kennel corridors themselves are important. A corridor which is too narrow can be difficult when manipulating cleaning equipment or when two people are working in the same kennel and passing each other in the corridor. A width of 130 cm is comfortable for easy working and cleaning. Some corridors have gullies (with or without gratings) to carry away excess cleaning water and often these are not deep enough to deal with the flow, so floods occur. Some purpose-designed manufactured units cater for a corridor only 90 cm wide and, in my opinion, this is not sufficient. One water point, or more in a really long building, is a necessity. A permanently attached hose is also useful in case of fire, but note the comments on water regulations in Chapter 6.

In addition to the runs attached to kennels, it is advantageous to have other larger and securely fenced runs where the dogs can run free occasionally (but see the previous discussion in Chapter 5). Grass or pebble surfaced runs need to be paved around the perimeter and at the entrance, both for tidiness and to deter escapees from tunnelling under the wire.

In wooden kennels, cat chalets or penthouses, there should be an inner lining which is treated with an impermeable, washable paint. Non-lead paints, of course, and no creosote for kennel or cattery woodwork. Creosote is toxic and takes ages to dry; it stains everything. Cuprinol is not harmful to dogs or cats, though the cedar colour may rub off a little onto light-coloured coats.

Chain-link fencing, which is usually used for the larger exercise runs, needs to be sunk in concrete below the ground surface, and the intervals between the supporting irons or posts should not be too great. Chain-link fencing is regularly advertised in the weekly dog papers by such firms as Jacksons, whose brochures describe both galvanised and green PVC-coated fencing. Outside perimeter fencing of chain link needs to have jump-deterring jackal-type fencing, ie taut wire strands sloping inwards atop 2-metre high chain link.

Boarding establishments which do not have attached covered runs to each individual kennel would find it extremely useful to have at least one outside covered exercise area, securely fenced, for use when the weather is doing its worst. Grass on outside runs needs periodic resting, and pebble surfaces can be changed occasionally. Pebble runs dry quickly after rain; many dogs enjoy and prefer grass as that is the normal surface for

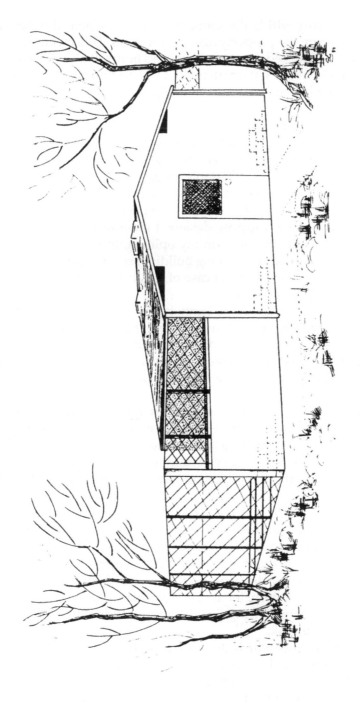

Purpose-built kennel block

Drawings courtesy of *Essential Kennel Design* by David Key

Typical Reception Layout (small)

Drawings courtesy of *Essential Kennel Design* by David Key

Barrack Block Kennels

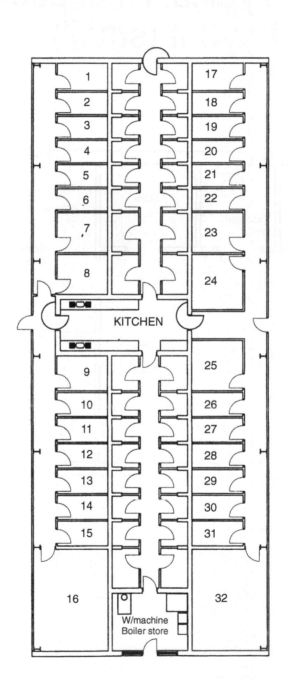

Drawings courtesy of *Essential Kennel Design* by David Key

Barrack Block (single)

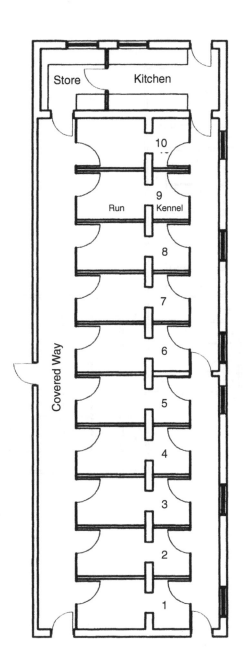

Drawings courtesy of *Essential Kennel Design* by David Key

Proposed new style Kennel

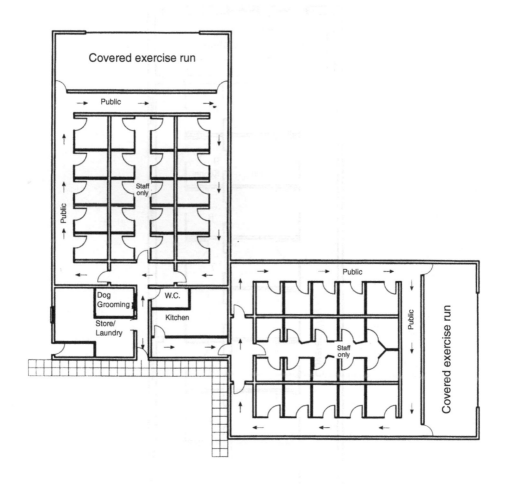

Drawings courtesy of *Essential Kennel Design* by David Key

Covered roof

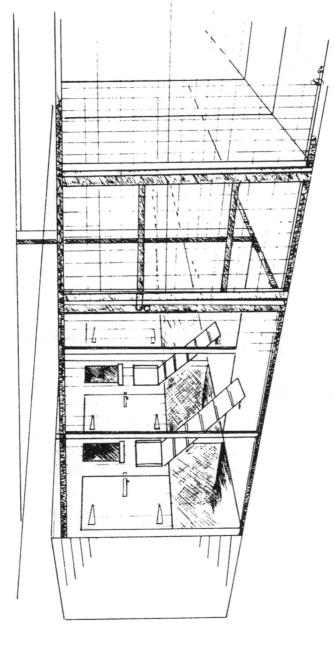

Penthouse cattery

Drawings courtesy of *Essential Kennel Design* by David Key

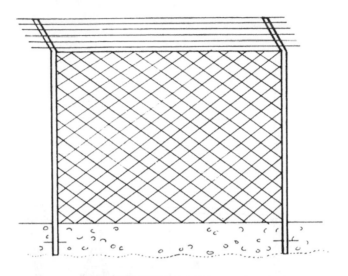

Security fencing

them at home, but keep the grass short or small dogs with long coats will get soaked after heavy dew or rain.

Isolation units

All kennels and catteries are required by law to have an isolation unit. This does not have to be extensive but separate units situated away from other boarders should be provided for dogs and cats and there should be accommodation for a few sick animals. (Note the points made on page 108.)

Walls

Kennel walls need to have an impermeable, easy to clean, surface. Breeze block walls need painting with a non-lead paint; an industrial one-coat cover-all emulsion is good, as the job has to be repeated frequently since regular wall washing and disinfecting, as well as scratching and chewing, takes a heavy toll of the decor. Breeze blocks with a smooth, impervious tile face remove the need for painting, as does the use of semi-engineering brick, but this adds to the capital costs. Always keep your eyes open for materials which will lessen your maintenance problems. The important points to remember when choosing a design or kennel plan are to be sure that (a) the building layout and materials are suitable under the Animal Boarding Establishments Act 1963, (b) they are easy to care for and (c) the boarders can be happy and comfortable in them.

Certain accident precautions should be borne in mind. For example, small mesh wire should be used for cat unit runs as chain-link would allow a cat's head to slip through and possibly become wedged. If the chain-link mesh used for kennel runs is too large, small dogs may try to get through and become stuck, sometimes with disastrous consequences. The purpose-made galvanised mesh panels used for kennel runs have many safety features.

Floors

Kennel floors need to be impermeable to water and other liquids. This usually means sealed concrete, though kennels for small dogs may be tiled – either with quarry tiles or, where damage by the occupants is likely to be negligible, with vinyl tiles. Toy dog breeds and cats are usually less hard on their surroundings, and some local authorities still approve wooden-floored buildings although they should not. Generally speaking, wooden kennel buildings are not recommended, even for cats these days, but this policy is one to discuss with the local authority as opinions vary.

Concrete floors need to be treated with a sealant or dust retardant. Raw concrete is not only dusty but is very porous and can harbour roundworm eggs. As urine and disinfectants can also penetrate porous concrete, it can become very smelly and unhygienic. Details of concrete sealers can be obtained from companies such as Compotect and Watco (Sales) Ltd. There are products for use on concrete outdoors and indoors, and it is important to use the right product in the right place. Concrete treatments are, unfortunately, not inexpensive and you should consult the industrial flooring experts for their advice, as the products themselves are not as easy to use as a tin of emulsion paint; in fact they can be very difficult, and professional application is advised.

Kitchens

The ideal is for each kennel building to have its own food storage, preparation and serving area, plus storage space for dishes and cleaning equipment. The food preparation area should be equipped with a hot water supply as well as cold – for washing dishes, obviously, and because disinfectants used in buckets of hot water are more efficient. There should also be at least a simple cooking arrangement, even if it is only a hotplate. As the ideal in this case is not very easy to find, consider whether you could make better arrangements than those shown to you when you are looking at kennels with a view to purchasing.

Gates

Kennel gates may vary from solid (in which case we are back to that 'shutting in the cupboard' position) to mesh or bars. One of the best kennel gate plans is one whose barred gates have a special device whereby water bowls are held in place (less spillage) and food bowls can be put into kennels without entering the kennel itself, both a time-saving device and very useful with difficult dogs. It is also a safety precaution to foil the quick escape artist! Solid partitions in a see-through material are also available; this is particularly useful when an impermeable barrier is required, as it is always desirable to see into a kennel and much more fun for the dogs if they can see out. Quarantine kennels and indoor catteries would find such equipment worth considering.

Radio

An extremely useful small appliance in the boarding kennel is the radio. Relatively inexpensive, probably filched from the household, it provides a touch of home from home and the sound of human voices, or music, for the dogs. It helps to keep some dogs quiet by distracting them from outside noises which might otherwise be the signal for a really good barking session.

HEATING

Some boarding kennels and quarantine kennels charge extra for heating. It would be safer to include it in the basic fees or a boarder's owner might well say the pet does not require heating when it really should have it, regardless of the fact that all your kennels are heated anyway.

Some kennels prefer to use only part of their complex during the winter, as bookings will be fewer and it is more economical to have part of the premises comfortably heated and well booked than to have some buildings with only one or two occupants needing warmth. Draught exclusion and insulation help to reduce heating costs.

Heating used in kennels must be safe and fume-free. Paraffin heaters and Calor gas stoves have too many potential dangers to leave unattended in any building, let alone in one used for animal housing. Central heating from an oil- or gas-fired boiler would prove ideal, but whether it is feasible to install such a heating unit depends on many things.

Electric, fan-assisted, warm-air heating, thermostatically controlled, is ideal, such as an Expelair. Some properties may be blessed with 'off peak' or 'white meter' electricity charges, which are a great advantage. However, these economy plans may not be suited to kennel use as the connected appliances do not start taking in heat until the middle of the night, and when they are giving off good heat it is time to open up the kennels and let out the dogs – and the heat too. Also, it can be extremely cold between 4 pm and 1 am in the depths of winter. Some other form of back-up heating would be necessary, so the system would not prove as economical in this context as it might in a purely domestic situation.

One of the most useful forms of kennel heating, for both dogs and cats, is the infra-red dull emitter lamp suspended over the sleeping area of the kennel or cat unit. The Wren Foster Ray dull emitter available from Diamond Edge is one of the best known of its kind and consists of a 'bulb' which gives warmth but no light, and looks rather like a small terracotta plant pot. It is available in various wattages and can be hung high or low in a kennel, out of reach of the dog. Heaters can be thermostatically controlled or fitted with a dimmer switch. Naturally, only the kennels which are occupied need to have the heater on. The clear red glass lamps which give both light and heat are more prone to breakage, or they may keep the dogs awake at night with resultant midnight barking, but at least you have a choice.

Other forms of electric heating used in kennels and catteries are the tubular greenhouse heaters, again attached to a thermostatic control. There are also electrically heated strong plastic beds available, and some heated pads for use in non-heated beds, though the latter devices are more suited to breeding kennels than to boarding kennels. Despite claims that the electrical connections are safe, one wonders if the makers have ever seen just how much damage a determined dog can do once it starts.

DEVELOPMENTS

It is important to be aware of any improvements you can make to your services – so long as your clients are prepared to pay for them. Recent innovations include 'luxury' kennels that boast television and video recorders on which the dog's favourite programmes can be played. Still more advanced is the provision of web cameras in each kennel, not just for the staff to keep an eye on the dogs but so owners can log on from anywhere in the world. It all sounds far fetched, but these services are already available in some kennels and clients are taking advantage of them – and paying for them!

11 Fanfare

Come blow your horn! You have purchased your boarding kennel, moved in and must advertise your presence. Advertising can cost a lot of money or relatively little, depending on who you are trying to attract to your business and how you set about the task.

TRADE SIGN

If yours is a domestic boarding business, as opposed to a quarantine kennel, it is most likely that the majority of your clients will come from your immediate area or within a radius of 10 to 15 miles. This is the area to saturate with regular advertising; the people need to know about you and the service you offer. To begin with, the 'Under New Management' tag attracts attention and if your kennel has a sign at the entrance, add it to this. 'Under new management' shows that you are neither sheltering behind your predecessor's goodwill nor are afraid to take up the challenge of building your own reputation. It may be necessary to consult the local authority planning department before a trade sign is erected, particularly if your property is down a country lane and you would like a directional sign on land which you do not own.

Have you ever considered a kennel logo, your very own trade mark? If there is someone in your family with artistic talent, make use of this and perhaps your own kennel logo will emerge and become an eye-catching symbol on your stationery and advertisements, on your car or van.

Pictures are remembered, and the simpler they are, the quicker they catch the eye.

ADVERTISING

Which local paper do most people in your catchment area read? The answer is, most probably, 'The paper that is delivered free!' Such papers are supported solely by advertising and your advertisement would be worth the investment in the classified column which caters for pets. You may also wish to try other local papers. The important thing is to monitor and log calls – 'May I ask where you heard about us?' – to ensure you are placing the advertisements where you are getting a return.

Your advertisements will of necessity be brief, but they should indicate whether you board dogs or cats, or only one genus, whether you give any additional service such as grooming, whether you specialise in large breeds – sufficient information to attract the attention and bring enquiries. A display advertisement in the local paper is usually the most advantageous, and your first might read something like the following:

BEERODE BOARDING KENNELS
(Under New Management)
SUPERIOR ACCOMMODATION
for
DOGS and CATS
Phone Beerode 1234 4321
www.beerodekennels.com

Smart advertising reaps rewards and not all of it need be in the form of paid insertions in newspapers. The aim should be to keep your business name in the public eye in as many ways as possible.

The Yellow Pages and Thompson Local Directories list dog and cat boarding establishments under 'Boarding Kennels'. If you bought an existing business, the telephone number should have been part of the deal, and still be in the Yellow Pages and Thompson Local Directories as well as the ordinary directory; the extra cost for a display advertisement will be a few hundred pounds. Find out if there are any other trade directories for your area. Is there a town guide? Many people are now used to the concept of 'shop local' so these small-scale small area directories are becoming increasingly well used.

Although the majority of your clients will come from the local catchment area, many people are willing to travel considerable distances to board their pets in a kennel, particularly a cattery, which is recommended or which they have used previously and found satisfactory. Plan advertising to cover this wider area.

A small advertisement occasionally in the specialist kennel magazine, *Kennel and Cattery Management*, or *Our Dogs*, *Dog World* or *Cats* will make your name known nationwide. Emphasise any specialised facilities you may have, such as reductions for several dogs from one kennel while the owner takes a holiday; whether you can take over someone's breeding kennel should the owner unfortunately become ill; whether your kennels are particularly suited to large breeds; whether you can offer specialist care for Tibetan breeds, Poodles, guard dogs, or whatever is your particular interest. Boarding needs are not confined only to the local pets whose owners are taking their annual vacation.

A further, and very important, medium for advertising your kennel is in publications and at locations concerned entirely with the armed forces. Many forces families are pet owners and the very nature of a forces career entails comings and goings and, therefore, the boarding of pets. If your kennel is situated anywhere near a service base, contact the relevant officer and ask about means of advertising your presence to forces families. Visit the local NAAFI store and note which forces magazines and newspapers are on sale and enquire about the advertising rates from the publishers.

Beware of advertising your kennels as an animal sanctuary, as this may imply that your business is a charity, which it is not. Avoid advertising that you take in rescued dogs. Yes, your kennel may well offer sanctuary to some pets on occasions, but you are running a business and official animal sanctuaries usually seek registered charity status.

Unfortunately, you may find that some people will consider your kennels as a sanctuary anyway; to put it more bluntly, some will look on your premises as a dumping ground for animals they no longer wish to keep. Word your advertisements to discourage this behaviour. This serious matter is also referred to in Chapter 5.

YOUR WEBSITE

Another advertising medium that you cannot ignore is the internet. You do not have to be a big business to have your own website and e-mail address. It is now fundamental to your business success. The key to a successful website is the 'link'. Your web page design can make use of a program that automatically circulates a number of key words and phrases to the search engines so that when a potential client searches for 'kennels anyshire uk', your website is listed early in the search (search engine optimisation). However, the most important link should be through the Yellow Pages. Yell.com (the electronic version of Yellow Pages) searches for businesses in any given area. If you have a link to your website at that point, the likelihood is that the searcher will log onto it. It is then easy for the person to make a booking by e-mail. The contact will throw up an e-mail address that you can add to your e-mail client list for marketing purposes, such as the circulation of reminders and special offers as they become available. As mentioned, a good website is now essential. You do not have to spend very much money – you will be surprised how inexpensively a series of web pages can be set up. There are several individuals and small companies within the world of dogs and cats that can design and post your site based on your brochure and include plenty of photographs of your premises. Membership of the Pet Care Trust will put your business (and web link and e-mail address) on their 'Find it' pages. People looking for a boarding kennel just have to key in their postcode and if it is in your county your name will come up. Google has introduced a series of schemes that are very helpful to small businesses. Get a Google account and work through the options, many of which are free.

If your advertising campaign works well and the bookings mount up, you will find that there are times when you are very busy indeed, and nice though this thought may be, be careful not to overbook. So often, everyone wants to bring the pet along on a Friday, but nobody wants to collect until Saturday, or even Monday. For this reason some kennels keep a 'change-over' kennel – a building which is not booked except to accommodate an overflow at such times. However, many boarding kennel owners would be quite happy if their only problems were concerned with accommo-dating an overflow of boarders.

Another tip is to only book 'full' weeks at busy times so that in August you do not take weekend or two- or three-day bookings.

TELEPHONE ENQUIRIES

When enquiries are mostly be made by phone, whoever answers must sound welcoming and be fully informed of boarding fees and services. The information must be kept in the office handy to the telephone.

You have to be your own salesman and 'sell' your kennel to the client. Ask for some special information about the caller's dog or cat, say something nice about the breed, or dogs and cats in general if the pet cannot claim to belong to any particular breed, build a little confidence, invite the caller to visit your kennels, by appointment of course. It is impossible to quote for grooming services to new clients until you have seen the dog: another reason to suggest a visit. Many owners think their pets have well-kept coats, but when the canine beautician starts to work on it, the amount of time needed to rescue the dog from its matted mantle may far outweigh the original estimate in time and money. Regular clients in the grooming department, if you have one, are a different matter altogether.

STATIONERY

You will probably be ordering new kennel stationery and handouts for prospective clients and need to consider what information you should include. Use the kennel logo and think whether it is best to say a lot or a little.

Your kennel stationery should include booking forms and brochures. These can be designed to suit your own needs and to tell your own story. Prospective clients will need a booking application form, either given to them when they visit the kennel or sent by post to enquirers. The booking form should be designed to establish all the information you need to know about the boarders and the owners, and contain some basic things they need to know about your kennels. It becomes a contract between you and the client and both parties are expected to honour the contract. As booking forms need to be filed in your office while the boarders are in residence with you, they have to be reasonably substantial, and they must be in duplicate so that both you and the pet owner have a copy. A sample booking application form is shown on page 53.

The brochure, which tells more about how you care for the dogs, is a handout you may want to use for general marketing and advertising purposes as well as for sending to clients with the booking form. Considerable care needs to be taken in preparing the brochure, which lists your conditions of boarding.

Your exact location, with a small map if necessary, should be shown, and your opening times should be clearly stated. It should list your boarding fees and any circumstances under which they may be altered. Any extras which the fees include – heating and insurance for example – should be mentioned. Your brochure should make it clear how your fees are applied; for example, if a dog arrives on Monday afternoon and departs the following Monday morning will you charge seven or eight days' fees? It should also be stated that fees are payable in advance or at the time of departure, that cheques will not be accepted without a banker's card and that no booking is guaranteed unless a deposit, non-returnable, is paid in advance. Make it known whether you are closed on bank holidays, and whether you are closed on one day during the week or have a half-day closing.

Make it quite clear that no animals are accepted to board unless they have a current certificate of vaccination against the most prevalent diseases and that absolutely no exception can be made for not presenting an up-to-date immunisation certificate. The health of your boarders and the reputation of your kennel depend on it.

Owners may be reminded that their pets are usually happier if they have their own beds and bedding (though you will have supplies for them if required) – it reminds the dogs of home. This is a terrible nuisance but both owners and their pets appreciate it. It is a good idea to encourage owners to bring their dog's towel, very useful in wet weather because the dogs will have to be dried after exercise. Mention whether you have a grooming service and make it clear whether it is a trimming and grooming service for all breeds or a simple brush and tidy up before the dogs go home. A full trimming service involves an extra charge, but a routine brush and combing should be inclusive.

State that you feed the dogs a well-balanced diet and use the best-quality food; make sure that you do! Let people know that the boarders' usual food will be taken into consideration. You could allow any owner to bring special supplies for the pet.

LOCAL ACTIVITIES

What else can you do? Become known in the local dog and cat show community even though you may not be an exhibitor and do not wish to become involved in either dog or cat breeding. Local breeders and exhibitors are often approached for recommendations to boarding kennels; they cannot recommend yours if they do not know anything about it or you. Contact your local canine society or cat club; the names of the secretaries can be obtained from the Kennel Club or the Governing Council of the Cat Fancy if you do not already know them. Find out if there is a ringcraft or obedience training class in your area. Go along to it, and take some brochures with you. These local societies will probably have a series of competitive events during the course of the year. Most of them are struggling along on a shoestring – you know the feeling! Offer a special prize or rosettes; a small investment, but your kennel name will appear on the literature: 'Best-in-Match Rosette presented by Beerode Kennels' – good advertising among people in a position to pass on your name to others. Take time out to go to the weekly ringcraft or obedience class, volunteer your services as a steward, offer to make the tea, just make yourself useful – and known in the local small animal community.

Local canine societies usually produce a newsletter – if they don't, suggest they start one, and lend a helping hand. Newsletters are great places for very inexpensive advertising, as are the societies' show schedules and catalogues. Of course, you will be very busy in the summer months, but shows and match meetings are held all the year round. They are friendly, enjoyable activities; helpers are always needed. In return for your help, or a donation towards rosettes, your name appears in the club literature.

In addition to mingling with the local professional dog and cat breeders and exhibitors, find out what general business organisations there are in your locality. You are the proprietor of a legitimate business and can meet other businessmen on equal terms. Besides, some of them are probably dog owners. You will be patronising their establishments; they in turn may patronise yours. Cultivate the other owner-operated businesses; the giant multiples are very impersonal. You can do a week's shopping in a hypermarket and never speak a word to anyone, although many now offer a noticeboard on which you can display a card advertising your services. Visit small traders and exchange the time of day; introduce yourself; be your own ambassador and sales executive. Local shops and newsagents often display small advertisement cards for a minimum charge: make use of these facilities.

Keep an eye on the local paper for news of what is going on at meetings of the parish and district councils. Are they making new by-laws about dogs? What about licensing? Are they complaining about dogs being a nuisance? Find out who is your representative and make sure you put him or her right on these doggy matters. Who is your Member of Parliament? Find out his or her views on new laws being considered concerning dog control and licensing; make your own reasoned views known. Your business may be at stake. Take an active part in community affairs. Yes, it will be hard to find the time, but if you do not stand up you may not be recognised.

Another good advertisement comes free of charge – free of extra charge anyway. You will need an estate car or a small van: see that it carries the name of your kennel, your logo if any, and your telephone number. Wherever you go around your neighbourhood the van can do your advertising for you. Park it in a prominent place; be sure the lettering is clear and easy to read and that the vehicle is always sparkling clean, as it reflects the image of your business.

Ask your local veterinary practice if your kennel name and address can be displayed on the notice board in their reception area. In fact, if you put your mind to it you may be able to think of several extra ways of keeping your kennel name in the public eye so that it will be remembered when somebody needs boarding accommodation for their pets.

Let it be known that visitors to your kennels are welcome, but insist on an appointment and make it quite clear that visitors, who may be future clients, do not touch any of the boarders. Not only may the visitors be carrying a few germs but the boarders may not want to be touched, and the visitors will be impressed with your care – whether for their safety or the dogs' matters not in this instance. Hopefully they will remember you when their pets, or their friends' pets, need boarding accommodation. With cats, the 'do not touch' regulation is mandatory. Only the cattery attendant or the owners touch the cats; they are much more easily subject to infections, and many can be lightning quick with a disapproving paw!

UNLICENSED COMPETITION

Having considered all possible ways of advertising your kennels, bear in mind that your very best advertisements are happy, well-cared-for dogs and cats, and satisfied owners. Remember, too, that other licensed boarding kennels in your area have every right to advertise their services, but keep a wary eye open for certain forms of unlicensed competition which are a threat to you and other licensed kennel operators too. There are people who advertise in the local paper or on postcards in shop windows, 'Your pets cared for in my home during your holidays', or some similar wording.

There is another form of direct competition from certain organisations or individuals who advertise that they will 'dog sit' in private homes while the owners are away, or will visit the property regularly to walk the dogs and feed them. Charges levied for these sitters' services are often higher than your professional fees would be and, of course, other people are using the owners' home facilities and there is no guarantee against burglary, despite advertised claims. There is, of course, no reason why a person should not look after a dog for a friend; however, if such services are advertised under the heading of 'boarding accommodation' or in any way imply that dog or cat boarding facilities are being offered, the licensed boarding kennel owner who uses the same advertising medium has good reason to complain to the publisher, as the legitimately licensed business has to fulfil certain stringent conditions of security and care and is paying for long-term advertising in the paper. You can make known to potential clients that dogs and cats are disturbed by their owners' absence. The pet left at an insecurely fenced private house may decide to leave and search for its own home. Pets suddenly finding different people inhabiting the home in its owner's place may be equally disturbed and act accordingly, possibly even resenting and becoming aggressive towards the strangers.

Private home boarding may undercut your prices. Place a postcard ad of your own, emphasising professional, approved and licensed kennels where pets are secure and cared for by trained staff.

Some of these services may be 'proper' businesses (see Chapter 13), but if they are not, they can undercut you. Do not hesitate to report them to your local authority.

12 Expanding Your Business

How to make the business more profitable is always in the mind of the boarding kennel owner who is trying to become established. Although it may be little comfort when things are slow, it is a proven fact that any business to do with small animal care grows on personal recommendation of satisfied clients. The bulk of your bookings will come in the recognised holiday months as so many pet-owning families have children, and school holidays dictate family vacation dates. Therefore, much of the repeat business is on an annual basis.

INCREASED CAPACITY

Perhaps the first thing to consider is that as some kennels have become established, they have found a need for more kennel accommodation. If you are considering adding some more dog kennels, why not research the sort of accommodation generally offered in your area? Are the really large breeds well catered for? Does anybody specialise in the toy breeds? Is there a kennel offering super luxury accommodation to the truly pampered pet? It is quite surprising that although most of the population want to find the cheapest boarding accommodation for their pets, there is a firm following for the luxury kennelling which is advertised infrequently. Infrequently? Is that a clue in itself? Perhaps your area could do with some five-star accommodation for discerning pets? All mod cons and personal radio.

Think very hard before you add a cattery to an existing dog boarding kennel. It is not ideal for the feline species to be boarded in close association with their canine brethren, but many pet owners have both dogs and cats. Some might look on it as the ideal expansion of the business because they believe a cattery means less work and more money. Do not believe that! It depends a great deal on the area in which your business is situated.

Before considering the addition of a cattery, find out how many other catteries there are in your area, how many are separate organisations and how many are run in conjunction with dog boarding establishments. Only too frequently a cat owner's attitude is to leave the cat in the care of a neighbour at holiday time and not bother with formal boarding; a wrong attitude, of course, but one which has an effect on your business.

GROOMING SERVICES

There is considerable interest at present in dog grooming and trimming – the work of the canine beautician. This is an all-year-round business except for a slack spell in January or February, though the first spring sunshine brings the clients back for trimming.

Before you think of starting a grooming service in conjunction with your kennels, consider whether you are trained for that particular job, or whether any member of your staff is an experienced canine beautician. Canine beauticians must be trained and it is not a job which can be learned from scratch on a very short course. Training can be very expensive, both from the point of view of tuition for the beginner and the cost of the equipment. It is also necessary to have a proper grooming room – which may perhaps double as a dispensary – a large bath with a shower spray and hot and cold water, of course. A large, very steady table is needed, and a good light. Perhaps most of all, it is important to realise that bathing, blow-drying, trimming and styling a dog takes time, and it is not a job which should have too many interruptions.

If you wish to offer a grooming service to existing clients, it would probably be considered an ancillary part of your kennel business and would not require 'change of use' permission. If you have not trimmed dogs before, you may wish to get in touch with the British Dog Groomers Association, which is part of the Pet Care Trust.

Should you not wish to take a training course yourself but would like to offer a trimming service, there may be a local canine beautician who would be prepared to work at your kennels on some arranged basis, or you may wish to employ a kennel staff member who is also a trained groomer. Either of these suggestions presupposes that you have a suitable grooming room and bathing facilities. Most trained trimmers own their personal equipment such as scissors and stripping knives.

Dogs such as Poodles and American Cocker Spaniels need trimming and bathing every six to eight weeks, and luxury coated breeds need a professional grooming at about the same interval of time, while Terriers and other Spaniel breeds need stripping two or three times a year. Thus you could have an interesting, and paying, ancillary business to your boarding kennel, and also a continuity of contact with your clients.

Although canine beauty equipment is quite expensive to buy, it lasts for years with regular care and servicing. Naturally, some grooming jobs are particularly hard on the equipment, *and* the groomer, for many people allow their Old English Sheepdogs or Afghans to become matted solid and such work is heavy and tiring. With perseverance you can encourage these wayward owners to become regular clients by a reminder telephone call and thus make life a lot better for the dogs, which are often very uncomfortable when their coats are full of mats and tangles.

PRODUCT SALES

People who board their dogs with you are a pet product purchasing population. A kennel owner is in a good position to advise on suitable types of collars and leads, feeding bowls, pet toys and pet foods, and sell them. Again, if these services are offered as an ancillary to your business, no official objections should be raised. However, if you wish to establish a fully fledged retail shop, consult the district authority first. Many councils restrict retail outlets to certain commercial areas.

A number of kennels sell foodstuffs to their clients, another continuing trade. Ask yourself if your kennel is situated in a good position for this to be a viable proposition, remembering the pet owner's tendency to buy the pet food along with the weekly groceries at the supermarket. So much depends on whether you have a good trading position and permission to open a 'Canine Cash and Carry'. However, remember that successful retailing depends on 'footfall' – the number of people you have access to. This is not very high within your premises; you could be holding a lot of stock that moves off the shelves only very slowly.

Should you decide not to become involved with ancillary trades at your kennel, you might look for other ways of keeping the kennels occupied. Sometimes boarding kennels are asked to accept police dogs – that is, their own dogs, not strays. If you have suitable kennels for large dogs, this may be a possibility. The police sometimes have dogs arriving for assessment and need extra accommodation for them. Contact your local constabulary on this matter.

Occasionally accommodation is required for guard dogs, and by charitable organisations for rescued dogs. Whether or not you will want to become involved with strays or rescued dogs (as they are likely not to have been inoculated) is questionable; you would be defeating your most important health rule in accepting such dogs.

Sometimes other kennel owners, either boarding kennel folk or the owners of breeding/exhibiting kennels, need to take a break. If you are prepared to offer a service to these people, an advertisement in the weekly dog press would be noticed, or if you are interested in a particular breed, try to keep a small running ad going in the breed club magazine. These latter advertisements are usually quite inexpensive and bring results.

PUPPY REARING

Many boarding kennel owners come into the business via the show world and may find they have extra income from puppy sales. However, much depends on the breed which is their particular interest and whether there is a demand for puppies. If you breed five or more litters a year, you will need a Breeding Licence under the Breeding of Dogs (Welfare) Act of 1999. Puppy rearing, if done properly, is a very time-consuming occupation, and is also very expensive. Profits are made only by cutting costs in every possible way, to the probable detriment of the puppies themselves. There is also the problem of disease, and many intensive puppy-breeding units were wiped out by canine parvovirus disease in the late 1970s and early 80s. Although there are now vaccines against this disease, baby pups are particularly vulnerable.

It is known that some boarding kennels have in the past bought in puppies from puppy farmers for resale locally. Resist this temptation. Buying in puppies in bulk is not impossible but you will need a separate pet shop licence and it is very difficult to retain your status and reputation if you are branded a puppy farmer or trader.

There is one service you might like to consider offering in your area… a special service to senior citizens. It is quite likely that older people would appreciate a break from the responsibility of their animal companions occasionally, perhaps while they visit relatives or maybe because they have to spend a few days in hospital. You could advertise special concessions for senior citizen pet owners at certain times. It would be better to offer such a service regularly, perhaps one week a month outside the peak periods, in order to keep a continuity of trade, contracts and recommendations flowing all the time. You may also be doing some pets a service too, as often their elderly owners forget to groom them, or maybe are unable to groom them or exercise the pets sufficiently.

QUARANTINE KENNELS

It should be clearly understood that quarantine kennels are not for people who have had no previous experience of dogs, although this aspect of kennel ownership may appear attractive and lucrative, and is an all-year-round trade. Considerable experience, preferably of domestic boarding kennel management, is necessary, though occasionally a quarantine establishment may be the first, and very successful, purchase for the owners. In such cases, the new owners may be taking on experienced staff, and may also have years of business experience in management and executive positions.

With the introduction and development of the Pet Travel Scheme the demand for quarantine accommodation has dropped sharply and many have let their quarantine status go and changed into regular boarding kennels.

However, fewer though these may be, there is still a demand and quarantine is a branch of the kennel business to which many aspire. If you have a boarding kennel which seems suitable for expansion in this way, what points should you consider? Dogs and cats, and certain other animals, which are brought into any part of the United Kingdom and Republic of Ireland must be imported under licence and serve six months' quarantine detention at a quarantine kennel approved by Defra in the UK or by the Department of Agriculture in the Republic of Ireland. Certain other countries, of which Australia and New Zealand are best known, will not import dogs and cats unless the animals have served their six months' quarantine in a rabies-free country such as ours, or unless they were born here or have lived here for a specified period of time. Therefore, there are many dogs and cats in our quarantine kennels which are in transit from another country to Australia or New Zealand. Once the six months' detention has been served, the dogs and cats remain on British soil in a non-quarantine environment – perhaps in the domestic section of the quarantine kennel – for a further specified time awaiting shipment to their future destinations. Obviously, quarantine kennels have a certain continuity of business which ordinary domestic boarding lacks.

Experienced owners of an existing domestic boarding business should consider carefully the suitability of their property and its location for quarantine purposes and should then contact their Divisional Veterinary Officer or one of the addresses given on page 146. Enquirers will receive full details concerning all aspects of operating a quarantine kennel, which will be subject to the control of the Ministry. The Ministry has detailed provisions for the design, construction, operation and management of authorised quarantine premises.

Planning permission will be needed from the local authority and an application must be made to Defra: no work on a proposed kennel should be undertaken until approval has been obtained in writing from both. A further requirement is that the owner shall nominate a Veterinary Superintendent who will undertake overall control of the premises, as the latter will be responsible to the Department for all aspects of the establishment. Quarantine establishments receive regular inspections on behalf of the Ministry and, of course, all requirements must be met or the licence may be jeopardised. Owners of quarantine kennels will be required to cooperate with any alterations in the regulations which may be deemed necessary by the Department according to changing circumstances; continuation of the licence will depend on the owner's ability to comply with changed regulations.

All the problems associated with dogs and cats coming into domestic boarding kennels are magnified considerably in quarantined animals which have probably made a long, and not altogether comfortable, air journey of many thousands of miles in a secure crate and then been driven to your kennel before being released… still to be deprived of a sniff at British grass for another six months! Stress on the animal is multiplied to an enormous degree, and the care which must be provided by the quarantine kennel staff is increased.

Show dogs are imported quite regularly and people who have worked overseas, particularly members of the armed forces, bring their pets home with them. In fact, one of the best ways of advertising quarantine accommodation is in the military magazines and newspapers. Of course, alongside quarantine business is shipping – importing and exporting – and naturally the 'Q' kennel needs to be a licensed carrier for quarantine-bound dogs and cats.

There have been some recent changes to our quarantine regulations, and there have also been suggestions that as rabies vaccines have been improved in recent years, quarantine regulations may eventually be abandoned altogether. This is not likely, although the number of countries from which dogs can be imported continues to increase and now numbers almost 100. Very many are islands that are known to be free of rabies, countries which are members of the European Union or countries which have acceptable rules governing rabies. The UK regulations are relatively straightforward but *must* be complied with. If they are not, the animal will be sent directly to a quarantine establishment on arrival in the UK.

To travel from the UK to another EU country, a pet must, in this order, be microchipped, vaccinated against rabies and issued with an EU Pet Passport. These requirements do not apply to pets travelling from the UK to the Republic of Ireland.

To enter or re-enter the UK from other EU countries without quarantine, a pet must, in this order, be microchipped, vaccinated against rabies and blood-tested, issued with an EU Pet Passport and treated against ticks and tapeworms. The pet must be more than three months old. After 28 days and before travelling, a blood test is carried out. If the results show that the pet has immunity, then it is allowed to travel. This must be within six months of the original vaccination, otherwise the owner has to start again. The animal is then able to be given a Pet Passport. These requirements do not apply to pets travelling to the UK from the Republic of Ireland.

This is just a summary. Full details, and they are extensive, can be down-

loaded from www.britischebotschaft.de/en/embassy/agriculture/pets_
factsheet.htm.

The reason for going into this detail is that one of the ways in which
quarantine kennels have expanded is by taking on the burden of this
administration on behalf of pet owners. Many earn more from ensuring
that all these details are properly completed, arranging laboratory tests
and veterinary visits and then transporting or collecting pets from the
designated ports of entry, than they do from boarding fees.

Whether the above relaxation of the quarantine regulations will be
further relaxed in view of improved vaccines, and some public opinion
which labels quarantine as 'cruel', remains to be seen. In these circumstances it would be wise for any boarding kennel owners who are considering adding quarantine accommodation to their present kennels, or
people purchasing a boarding kennel which already has quarantine
accommodation, to contact their Divisional Veterinary Officer or the office
of Defra for their area for the latest information, as changes in quarantine
regulations obviously affect the boarding kennel business.

Enquiries concerning quarantine kennels should be addressed to your
Divisional Veterinary Officer, whose address may be obtained from your
own veterinary surgeon, or to:

Defra
www.defra.gov.uk – a useful website that lists all the contact details for
Animal Health divisional offices.
For information on any aspect of Defra's work, contact the Defra
helpline, tel: 08459 335577, e-mail: helpline@defra.gsi.gov.uk.

Department of Agriculture and Fisheries for Scotland
is now SOAEFD: Scottish Office Agriculture, Environment and Fisheries
Department.

**www.scotland.gov.uk/Topics/Agriculture/animal-
welfare/News/8377#a4**
has an extensive contact list for Animal Health divisional offices across
Scotland, England and Wales.

Department of Agriculture (Ireland)
Head Office -- Agriculture House, Kildare Street, Dublin 2; lo-call 1890
200 510, also 607 2000.

http://agriculture.gov.ie/printindex.jsp?file=contact.xml
for an index of Irish contacts.

The Ministry of Agriculture, Fisheries and Food for Northern Ireland
is now part of Defra.

Animal Health (Agency)
Corporate Centre
C11 Government Buildings
Whittington Road
Worcester
WR5 2LQ
Tel: 01905 767111 (office hours only)
Fax: 01905 768851
E-mail: corporate.centre@animalhealth.gsi.gov.uk
Website: www.defra.gov.uk/animalhealth/index.htm

13 Associated Services

INTRODUCTION

From the mid-1970s to the turn of the century, the number of dogs within the UK gradually declined from about 7.5 million to about 5 million. At the same time the number of cats increased from about 6 million to over 7 million. The reasons for this change are many and varied. They include the fact that many more people are living in single accommodation where keeping a pet is more difficult, or in smaller properties with tiny or non-existent gardens, as well as the increase both in leisure time and in the variety of leisure activities. The national media, too, have played their part, and health issues, fear of disease and, in the case of dogs, biting have featured regularly.

The pet industry, through the major pet food manufacturers and the Pet Care Trust (which represents professional retailers, manufacturers, groomers and kennels and catteries), has fought back with, in the past 10 years, the support of charities such as Dogs Trust and Blue Cross and organisations such as the Kennel Club. It is in their interests, of course, but the basis of the campaign has been that pets are good for people and that there are many sound educative and social reasons for pet ownership. People who own pets live longer and go to the doctor less often, and their children go to school more regularly. You can get the details and research that backs it up from www.petcaretrust.org.uk, where, if you click onto the 'Pets are Good for You' link, you are directed to the publication that summarises all this material. The result has been that the decline in dog ownership appears to have been halted and the ownership of other pets, particularly rabbits, has continued, overall, to increase.

Part of the reason has been that while people want to own a pet, they have more money and can afford to pay for others to look after them. A parallel can be drawn with the rapid increase in the number of nannies employed and the play and nursery facilities that have opened. It can be more economical for both members of the household to work and pay others to look after their children. The same has happened within the pet industry: there has been an explosion of ancillary services providing support for families and single people with pets. And the sector is substantial. There are believed to be over 3,000 pet sitters and dog walkers in the UK, some of whom are clearly earning an extra few pounds a week 'on the side', but many have a fully fledged business and employ a team of walkers and sitters. Others, such as PetPals, have launched franchises, imparting their expertise to others for a fee.

These services are in direct competition with the established boarding kennel sector. They are largely unregulated and have minimal capital costs, so can undercut by a significant amount the standard fees charged by traditional boarding kennels. In fact, this appears not to happen, and 'care' costs for animals on a daily basis are not very different from the full-rate fees charged by kennels, so they remain relatively competitive. This is partly because the small individual trader cannot cope with as many animals as a well-run kennel, so fees have to be higher if a living income is to be earned. However, kennel proprietors are bound to feel that money is going into the pockets of 'fly-by-nights' rather than into their own.

There is no point in worrying about it. We live in a society which allows people to set up whatever business they choose so long as it is within the law, and most of these services neither require registration nor are subject to regulation.

And there are opportunities for kennel owners too, so those considering owning their own kennels should read this chapter carefully. To know the extent of your competition is valuable in itself.

Finally, ancillary services remain a part of the pet industry. They may be competition for established businesses but they have a role to play, and if they can be persuaded to play a full part in the industry through member-ship of the Pet Care Trust, they will have access to recognised standards and codes of practice, which in the long run will benefit pets, their owners and the industry as a whole.

PET SITTING AND DOG WALKING

For many years, Animal Aunts provided a home sitting service for people who were going on holiday and did not want to put their pets into kennels. It certainly did not save money, because any full-time service is expensive. But it had several advantages: several pets could be looked after, including the goldfish, and having the family home occupied avoided leaving the house completely unattended for any length of time.

Animal Aunts works like an employment 'agency', so the people used are self-employed. An agency fee of 25 per cent is charged and they mainly use retired people, require excellent references and have built up a good reputation. There are now several organisations which work in the same way.

Most pet sitters who have come into the market over the past few years are also independents. Many belong to the National Association of Pet Sitters (NARP), which has a 'find it' service for the general public and provides a code of practice and some distance learning training for its members. It also advocates 'home boarding' – but more of that later.

One of the main concerns of the 'professional' pet sector is that pet sitters and dog walkers need have no training. Anyone with a few hours to spare can pop into someone's house and let the dog out, feed the cat and charge for the service. It sounds like easy money, and it is until something goes wrong. The fees are almost always paid in cash or the occasional cheque and then disappear into the black economy. Anyone running such a service as a business should realise that, as in any competitive enterprise, local 'proper' traders will resent them and are likely to ring one of the government's 'report lines', which are used for the anonymous reporting of benefit or income tax fraud. They should therefore be properly registered and listed by the Pet Care Trust, NARP or one of the other professional organisations in the field. They should also have a bank account and an accountant to ensure they are working within the law, and should take out professional liability insurance.

Just as important, they should ensure that they understand their responsibilities to their employers and the pets they look after. Just having pets of their own does not give anyone enough relevant experience to take on these responsibilities. The advice given in this book about the management of a business is just as relevant to the sole, small trader as it is to a more complex organisation and it is worthy of careful study.

The provision of a top-quality, professional service will bring in business. A sloppy, slovenly approach will inevitably run the risk of serious problems arising.

Pet sitters and dog walkers should have a thorough grounding in the care of animals in the home environment. They should be aware of the basic legislation concerning pets and understand the fundamentals of advertising and marketing, and the importance of business and financial records, banking procedures and taxes. A thorough understanding of health issues affecting pets found in the home – and remember that as well as dogs, these can include fish, reptiles and a whole range of 'small and furries' – is essential. Handling and restraint are also important skills, as is a knowledge of the range of infectious diseases which may be encountered. Much of this material is covered in earlier chapters, but the pet sitter will come into contact with a much wider range of species. The Animal Care College provides a special course for pet sitters which covers both the care of pets and the development of the business.

Those pet sitters and walkers who can show their commitment to good business practice will greatly benefit both in the custom they attract and the fees they can charge. For instance, the most sensible way to find those first customers is to advertise the service by means of a postcard in the window of a local newsagent or a classified advertisement in the local paper. How much greater your credibility must be if the advertisement can say 'Fully insured and qualified through the Animal Care College'. Another sensible investment is in a properly printed, numbered receipt book. Not only will this impress your clients, but it will be a boon to your accountant.

There are few restrictions on the sole trader. When you first set up the business you must inform HM Revenue & Customs (HMRC) that you are self-employed. You can find more information about how to do this, including a form you can use to notify HMRC about your business at www.businesslink.gov.uk.

You will also need to fill in a self-assessment tax return. The latest submission date for tax returns is 31 January each year (for the preceding financial year – that is, your return for the financial year April 2008 to April 2009 must be in by the end of January 2010). This is very helpful to very small businesses because you do not have to pay until almost a year later (and the payments are half and half, six months apart), but bad news if you have spent all the money. (Make sure you put some aside for tax and National Insurance.) There are financial penalties for late submission.

If you take on staff, you will have the additional responsibility of deducting Income Tax and Class 1 National Insurance Contributions from their pay, and paying it along with your Employer's Contribution to HMRC, under the Pay As You Earn scheme. For more information, see Chapter 9. To download a copy of the guidance leaflet and the necessary registration forms go to www.hmrc.co.uk.

Much of the preceding information applies to dog walkers, but they have a broader social responsibility which does not affect pet sitters. Most dog walkers have contracts with several different owners and it is clearly convenient for them to take several dogs out for a walk at the same time. If they only work within a restricted area, it may be possible for them to collect dogs and drop them off on the way round a reasonable 'circuit', but this ideal situation seldom occurs. Houses tend to be in streets, and dog walking really requires open spaces – and ones where dog walking is allowed. Many dog walkers need a vehicle and this brings its own complications. Dogs must be kept apart when the walker is not present to be 'in control'. In unusual or frightening surroundings a dog's natural reaction is to defend its space, and fights are an inevitable consequence. Separate cages or boxes are a necessity, apart from the fact that dogs can easily get loose if they are not kept in separate cages or boxes.

Moving dogs into and out of boxes and vehicles is an art in itself, for although many dogs are well behaved and will come when called even by a relative stranger, this is not to be relied upon. The business of safe collars and leads, ensuring that all leads are in your hand but that the dogs have enough room to stay out of each other's space, is a skill which takes time to learn. It is difficult to place a figure on the number of dogs that can be walked safely at any one time because the circumstances are so varied. Ten toy dogs may be easy to manage and well behaved: a Rottweiler and two Great Danes can be too many for even an experienced handler.

Consideration must also be given to clearing up on the walk. Walking several well-behaved dogs may not be a problem, but managing to hold onto them while you scoop the poop – often a tricky operation even with just one dog – can be impossible.

Care must always be taken not alarm the general public. Dog walkers tend to find suitable places to walk their charges and it is likely that several will be in the same area at the same time. It is not surprising if they stop for a chat – but suddenly you have 30 dogs milling about. Apart from the risk of biting and fighting, such a group can be very intimidating to others using the same area. At the moment there are no regulations concerning dog walking, but several local authorities are introducing by-laws to cope with what they see as a serious problem within their boundaries. Also, the new Animal Welfare Bill has enabling clauses within it which will allow Defra to impose regulations if the government feels it to be necessary.

Like pet sitting, dog walking is viewed with suspicion by the boarding kennels and cattery industry. There is no real need for concern. The majority of pet dogs and cats never see the inside of a boarding kennel anyway (estimates vary between 60 and 80 per cent), so there is an untapped market not currently being exploited by kennel owners. Moreover, these ancillary services are making it easier for the general public to own pets, so in that sense they are making a genuine contribution to the industry.

CRÈCHES

There is a halfway house between boarding and pet sitting. This is the crèche. A number of crèches have sprung up recently run by veterinary surgeries, ex-veterinary nurses or experienced kennel staff, and many have been very successful. It is an opportunity which boarding kennel owners should explore. Many have taken in boarders on a day basis, but a crèche does much more. Staff are employed to 'play' with the dogs through the day, sand pits and play equipment are available and small kennels are provided for the dogs to have an 'afternoon rest'. There are some worries here in that such premises have been obtaining boarding licences quite against the provisions of the Model Licence Conditions (safety features and the 'mixing' of dogs belonging to different owners, to name but two), but so far there have been few problems. A safe barn or even a little-used church hall or sports pavilion is all that is needed.

The charges for such facilities are high for they are labour intensive, but if there is a demand, there is no doubt that forward-thinking entrepreneurs with experience of pet care will fulfil it. The business demands and requirements remain the same as for any small business, but it seems to me that a crèche would be a very useful extra income stream for any boarding kennel.

HOME BOARDING

Home boarding – where someone uses their own home and garden to look after the pets of others – is a problem. If it is anything other than a cat or dog, no problem exists, but if it is a dog or cat the premises are subject to the Animal Boarding Act of 1963 and they should fulfil all the Model Licensing Conditions as set out in previous chapters. In my view it is not possible for an ordinary home to fulfil those conditions, but many local authorities are ignoring home boarding or licensing homes for, usually, up to six dogs. There are often other conditions too (perhaps all the pets must be from the same family or premises), but the fundamental requirements of the Act are still being flouted.

Home boarders tell me how careful they are, how they only take on dogs that are reliable, friendly and do not want to escape, and how much their clients appreciate their pets being looked after in a true home environment. But they often have no training, the house is busy, children go in and out all day and they may be leaving the dogs alone while they shop, pet-sit or walk dogs for other clients. Such premises cannot be considered safe for looking after animals which belong to other people.

Final Note

Running a boarding kennel or cattery or working in any capacity with pets is not for everyone, and reading through this manuscript I am conscious that I have been fairly downbeat about many aspects of the sector. Many of those taking the Diploma of Kennel Management have told me that it was the best value for money they have ever had, 'because it showed me that this was *not* something I wanted to do'.

The same thinking applies to this book. If it helps you make up your mind, either way, it will have achieved its purpose. If it is helpful if you do decide to go ahead, that will be better still. You will be providing a valuable and much-appreciated service to your local community and really will 'be your own boss'.

I was involved in running kennels for many years and never regretted a moment of it. I leave you on that optimistic note. Good luck.

Appendix A

Early editions of *Running Your Own Boarding Kennels* have an extensive list of suppliers' addresses and other useful information for boarding kennel owners. The problem with such a list is that in a rapidly changing world, companies go out of business, merge or move and organizations change their names, locations and telephone numbers. Remember that your local phone book lists many of the services you will need and includes the telephone numbers and addresses of your local authority (for VAT and other tax enquiries), the local Health and Safety office, and the local Veterinary Officer, Chamber of Commerce, Business Link and Learning and Skills Council.

These days most owners of kennels will own a computer and be connected to the internet and may be using it in the day-to-day running of their business. Many of the established information sites will have e-mail addresses and a dedicated website and these are given in the text where available. At the same time, there are few products or services available that cannot be tracked down using one of the intelligent search engines such as Google, or through the Yellow Pages online service – Yell.com.

Any kennel owner will often need to refer to companies and organisations for estimates, quotes and advice and will need to obtain relevant telephone numbers and addresses rapidly. Even with access to the internet, to have the widest range of choice in the animal care sector, three paper publications are essential. All are updated each year and between them they should supply most of the data required. They are:

The *Pet Care Trust Year Book,* supplied free to members but at a fee for non-members, lists all members and related animal care organisations under a range of headings. It is published in July each year. Contact Info@petcare.org.uk and see www.petcare.org.uk.

The *Crufts Official Guide* (*not* the show catalogue) lists all the trade stands exhibiting at the show (between 300 and 400) and is available for purchase at the show, which is held at the National Exhibition Centre, or can be ordered around March each year from the Kennel Club. See www.the-kennel-club.org.uk.

The *Catalogue of the National Cat Show,* which is held at Olympia in December each year, lists all the details of the trade stands that are exhibiting. See www.nationalcatclub.co.uk.

Other useful publications:

Our Dogs and *Our Cats,* 1 Lund Street, Trafford Park, Manchester M16 9EJ
Tel 0870 731 6503, www.ourdogs.co.uk
Our Dogs has one of the most extensive and informative websites on the internet and provides links as well as web design and hosting for the animal care industry. Kennels and catteries are often offered for sale privately through its classified columns. The *Our Dogs* and *Our Cats Annuals,* published in December of each year, are mines of information about the canine and feline world.

Dog World, Somerfield House, Wotton Road, Ashford, Kent TN23 6LW
Tel 01233 621877, fax 01233 645669, www.dogworld.co.uk
Kennels and catteries are often offered for sale privately through its classified columns. *The Dog World Annual,* published in December of each year, contains much useful information about the canine world.

Kennel and Cattery Management, Albatross Publications, PO Box 523, Horsham, West Sussex RH12 4WL
Tel 01293 871201, fax 01293 871301, www.kennelandcattery.com
Contains many features and updates on all matters affecting kennels and catteries.

Pet Business World News, 6 The Rickyard, Clifton Reynes, Olney, Buckinghamshire MK46 5LQ
Tel 01234 714404, e-mail info@pbwnews.com

Pet Product Marketing, EMAP Apex, Apex House, Oundle Rd, Peterborough, PE2 9NP
Tel 01733 898100, fax 01733 890657

Essential Kennel Design, David Key (available direct from *Our Dogs*).

Your Dog, Dogs Today, Dogs Monthly and *Cat World* are available through your local newsagent.

Other important addresses:

The Animal Care College, Index House, High Street, Ascot, Berkshire SL5 7EU.
Tel 0845 123 8362, fax 0845 123 8361, e-mail info@rtc-mail.org.uk, www.animalcarecollege.co.uk
The college provides a range of distance learning (correspondence courses) on all aspects of kennel work, kennel management and understanding animals.

The College of Animal Welfare, London Road, Godmanchester, Huntingdon, Cambridgeshire PE29 2LJ
Tel 0870 062 1122, fax 0870 062 1133, e-mail admin@caw.ac.uk
The college provides a wide range of short courses on many aspects of kennel work and management.

Chartered Institute of Environmental Health, Chadwick Court, 15, Hatfields, London SE1 8DJ
Tel 020 7928 6006, fax 020 7827 5865
cieh@cieh.org.uk, www.cieh.org.uk

The following companies specialise in kennel and cattery properties:

The Kennels Agency, Moorfield House, Mattishall Road, Dereham, Norfolk NR20 3BS
Tel 01362 698855, fax 01362 698100, e-mail Ledoghouse@tesco.net
enquiries@thekennelsagency.co.uk, www.thekennelsagency.co.uk

Kennel Sales, Ladybird Kennels, Roman Road, Ingatestone, Essex CM4 9AD
Tel 01277 356641, fax 01277 356643,
wwwkennelsforsale.co.uk

Keltic Business Transfer, PO Box 218, East Horsley, Leatherhead, Surrey KT24 5YQ
Tel 0845 006 0841, fax 0845 006 0842
www.kbtassociates.co.uk, info@kbtassociates.co.uk

Appendix B

NATIONAL PET-RELATED ORGANISATIONS

ANIMAL HEALTH TRUST
Lanwades Farm
Kentford
Suffolk
CB8 7UU
Tel: 01638 751000
Fax: 01638 555606
Website: www.aht.org.uk

**ASSOCIATION FOR THE STUDY
OF REPTILIA & AMPHIBIA**
Natural History Museum
Cromwell Road
London
SW7 5BD

**ASSOCIATION OF PET
BEHAVIOUR COUNSELLORS**
PO Box 46
Worcester
WR8 9YS
Tel: 01386 751151
Fax: 01386 751151

**ASSOCIATION OF PET DOG
TRAINERS**
PO Box 17
Kempsford
GL7 4WZ
Tel: 01285 810811
E-mail: apdtoffice@aol.com
Website: www.apdt.co.uk
Enclose an s.a.e. please

BLUE CROSS
Shilton Road
Burford
Oxon
OX18 4PF
Tel: 01993 822651
Fax: 01993 823083
E-mail: info@bluecross.org.uk
Website: www.bluecross.org.uk

BRITISH CHELONIA GROUP
PO Box 1176
Chippenham
Wiltshire
SN15 1XB

**BRITISH HEDGEHOG
PRESERVATION SOCIETY**
Hedgehog House
Duhstone
Ludlow
Shropshire
SY8 3PL
Tel: 01584 890801

**BRITISH HERPETOLOGICAL
SOCIETY AND YOUNG
HERPETOLOGICAL CLUB**
11 Strathmore Place
Montrose
Angus
DD10 8LQ
Tel: 020 8452 9578
Website: www.thebhs.org.uk

BRITISH HORSE SOCIETY
Stoneleigh Deer Park
Kenilworth
Warwickshire
CV8 2XZ
Tel: 01926 707700
E-mail: enquiry@BHS.org.uk
Website: www.bhs.org.uk

**BRITISH SMALL ANIMAL
VETERINARY ASSOCIATION**
Woodrow House
1 Telford Way
Waterwells Business Park
Quedgeley
Gloucester
GL2 4AB
Tel: 01452 726700
Fax: 01452 726701
E-mail:
customerservices@bsavastore.com
Website: www.bsavastore.com

**BRITISH VETERINARY
ASSOCIATION**
7 Mansfield Street
London
W1G 9NQ
Tel: 0207 636 6541
Fax: 0207 436 2970
E-mail: bvahg@bva.co.uk
Website: www.bva.co.uk

**BRITISH VETERINARY NURSING
ASSOCIATION (BVNA)**
82 Greenway Business Centre
Harlow Business Park
Harlow
Essex
CM19 5QE
Tel: 01279 408644
Fax: 01279 408645
Website: www.bvm.org.uk

CANINE PARTNERS
Mill Lane
Heyshott
Midhurst
West Sussex
GU29 0ED
Tel: 08456 580480
Fax: 08456 580481
Website: www.caninepartners.co.uk

**CHILDREN IN HOSPITAL AND
ANIMAL THERAPY
ASSOCIATION (CHATA)**
Sandra Stone
87 Longland Drive
Totteridge
London
N20 8HN
Tel: 0208 445 7883
Fax: 0208 445 7883

COMPANION ANIMAL WELFARE COUNCIL (CAWC)
The Dene
Old North Road
Bourne
CB3 7TZ
Tel: 01954 718882
Website: www.cawc.org.uk

DOGS FOR THE DISABLED
Francis May Centre
Blacklocks Hill
Banbury
Oxon
OX17 2BS
Tel: 01295 252600
E-mail: info@dogsforthedisabled.org.uk
Website:
www.dogsforthedisabled.org.uk

DOGS TRUST
17 Wakely Street
London
EC1V 7LT
Tel: 020 7837 0006
E-mail:
customerservices@dogstrust.co.uk
Website: www.dogstrust.org.uk

FELINE ADVISORY BUREAU
Taeselbury
High Street
Tisbury
Wiltshire
SP3 6LD
Tel: 01747 871872
Fax: 01747 871873
Website: www.fabcats.org

THE GOVERNING COUNCIL OF THE CAT FANCY
5 Kings Castle Business Park
The Drove
Bridgwater
Somerset
Tel: 01278 427575
Website: www.gccfcats.org.uk

THE GUIDE DOGS FOR THE BLIND ASSOCIATION
Hillfields
Burghfield Common
Reading
RG7 3YG
Tel: 0118 983 5555
Fax: 0118 983 5433
E-mail: guidedogs@guidedogs.org.uk
Website: www.guidedogs.org.uk

HEARING DOGS FOR DEAF PEOPLE
Wycombe Road
Saunderton
Princes Risborough
Buckinghamshire
HP27 9NS
Tel: 01844 348100
Fax: 01844 348101
Website: www.hearing.dogs.org.uk

THE KENNEL CLUB
(Breed Rescue Society Information)
1 Clarges Street
Piccadilly
London W1J 8AB
Tel: 0870 60 66750
Website: www.the-kennel-club.org.uk

NATIONAL DOG WARDEN ASSOCIATION (NDWA)
Sue Bell
NDWA
Hatfield Lodge
Gloucester Road
Corse
Staunton
Gloucestershire
GL19 3RA
E-mail: sbell@NDWA.co.uk
Website: adwa.co.uk

NATIONAL OFFICE OF ANIMAL HEALTH LTD (NOAH)
3 Crossfield Chambers
Gladbeck Way
Enfield
Middlesex
EN2 7HF
Tel: 020 8367 3131
Fax: 020 8363 1155
E-mail: noah@noah.co.uk
Website: www.noah.co.uk

ORNAMENTAL AQUATICS TRADE ASSOCIATION (OATA)
Wessex House
40 Station Road
Westbury
Wiltshire
BA13 3JN
Tel: 08700 434013
Website: www.ornamentalfish.org

PEOPLE'S DISPENSARY FOR SICK ANIMALS (PDSA)
Head Office
Whitechapel Way
Priorslee
Telford
Shropshire
TF2 9PQ
Tel: 01952 290999
Fax: 01952 291035
Website: www.pdsa.org.uk

PET ADVISORY COMMITTEE (PAC)
Westminster Strategy
1 Bedford Avenue
London
WC1B 3AU
Tel: 020 7255 5475

PET FOOD MANUFACTURERS' ASSOCIATION (PFMA)
20 Bedford Street
Covent Garden
London
WC2E 9HP
Tel: 020 7379 9009
Fax: 020 7379 8008
Website: www.pfma.org.uk

PET HEALTH COUNCIL
20 Bedford Street
Covent Garden
London
WC2E 9HP
Tel: 020 7379 6545
E-mail:
enquiries@pethealthcouncil.co.uk
Website: www.pethealthcouncil.co.uk

PETS AS THERAPY
3a Grange Farm Cottages
Wycombe Road
Saunderton
Princes Risborough
Buckinghamshire
HP27 9NS
Tel: 08144 345445
Website: www.petsastherapy.org.uk

ROYAL COLLEGE OF VETERINARY SURGEONS
Belgravia House
62–64 Horseferry Road
London
SW1X 8QP
Tel: 020 7222 2001
Fax: 020 7222 2004
E-mail: admin@rcvs.org.uk
Website: www.rcvs.org.uk

SOCIETY FOR COMPANION ANIMAL STUDIES (SCAS)
(see Blue Cross)

SUPPORT DOGS
21 Jessops Riverside
Brightside Lane
Sheffield
S9 2RX
Tel: 0114 261 7800
Fax: 0114 261 7555
Website: www.supportdogs.org.uk

UNIVERSITIES FEDERATION FOR ANIMAL WELFARE (UFAW)
The Old School
Brewhouse Hill
Wheathampstead
Hertfordshire
AL4 8AN
Tel: 01582 831818
Fax: 01582 831414
E-mail: ufaw@ufaw.org.uk
Website: www.ufaw.org.uk

WWF
Education Department
Panda House
Weyside Park
Godalming
Surrey
GU7 1XR
Tel: 01483 426444
Fax: 01483 426409
E-mail: supporterrelations@wwf.org.uk
Website: www.wwf.org.uk

Further Reading

A wide range of animal related titles are available through *Our Dogs*, which would be pleased to send you a full list. Telephone 0870 731 6502, or you can order online at www.ourdogs.co.uk

Additional Kogan Page titles for small businesses are:

The Business Plan Workbook, 6th edition (2008) by Colin Barrow, Paul Barrow and Robert Brown
Financial Management for the Small Business, 6th edition (2006) by Colin Barrow
How to Market your Business, 6th edition (2008) by Dave Patten
How to Prepare a Business Plan, 5th edition (2008) by Edward Blackwell
Law for the Small Business, 12th edition (2007) by Patricia Clayton
Starting a Business from Home, (2008) by Colin Barrow
Starting a Successful Business, 6th edition (2008) by Michael J Morris

Also recommended are the following Feline Advisory Bureau publications:

Boarding Cattery Construction and Management, S M Hamilton-Moore
Chemical Disinfection in the Cattery, P J Johnson, BVSc, MRCVS
Domestic Toxic Hazards to Cats, Sarah A Wilkins, BVSc, MRCVS
Zoonoses, A I Wright, BVSc, MRCVS

Especially recommended is David Key's standard work on kennel construction, *Essential Kennel Design*. David Key, like the author of this book, David Cavill, acts as a consultant to kennel owners. David Key concentrates on construction and planning; David Cavill concentrates on management, development and relations with local authorities.

Index

Index of Advertisers

Lightning Source UK Ltd.
Milton Keynes UK
UKHW02f0728050718
325255UK00004B/141/P